Murray Schisgal · Thornton Wilder
Tennessee Williams · Edward Albee

# Great American One-act Plays

## Model Interpretations

by Irene Jansen
and Stephen W. Souris



Ernst Klett Verlag

Lehrerbuch von Irene Jansen, Schwabbach, und Stephen W. Souris, Madison, Wisconsin (*Content* und *Teaching Units:* Irene Jansen; *Analysis:* Stephen W. Souris und Irene Jansen)
unter Mitwirkung der Redaktion Neue Sprachen.
Mitarbeit an diesem Werk: Dr. Hartmut K. Selke, Verlagsredakteur.

Schülerbuch herausgegeben von Stephen W. Souris.

## Acknowledgments

Murray Schisgal, *The Pushcart Peddlers,* copyright © 1981 by Murray Schisgal, from *The Best Short Plays* 1981 and Tennessee Williams, *The Last of My Solid Gold Watches,* copyright © 1945, 1953, 1981 by Tennessee Williams, from *The Theatre of Tennessee Williams,* Vol. 6 (1981) are reprinted by permission of International Creative Management, Inc., New York.

Edward Albee, *The Zoo Story,* copyright © 1959 by Edward Albee, is reprinted by permission of Stefani Hunzinger Bühnenverlag GmbH, Bad Homburg.

Thornton Wilder, *The Happy Journey to Trenton and Camden,* copyright © Thornton Wilder, 1959, from *The Long Christmas Dinner and Other Plays in One Act* (1931), is reprinted by permission of Paul und Peter Fritz AG, Zürich, acting on behalf of The Estate of Thornton Wilder.

The plays to which these interpretations refer are also available in a students' edition: *Great American One-act Plays* (Klettbuch 57821). The texts of Schisgal's *The Pushcart Peddlers* and Williams' *The Last of My Solid Gold Watches* (Cassette 1, Klettnummer 57823) and Albee's *The Zoo Story* (Cassette 2, Klettnummer 57824) are also available on cassette.

ISBN 3-12-578220-1

1. Auflage 1 5 4 3 2 | 1989

Die letzte Zahl bezeichnet das Jahr dieses Druckes.

Umschlaggestaltung: Hans Lämmle, Stuttgart.
Druck: Gutmann & Co., Heilbronn. Printed in Germany.

# Contents

# Preface

This collection of one-act plays deals with many aspects of American life. At the core, however, the plays are concerned with the whole range of the American experience: From the hope of the immigrants in Schisgal's *The Pushcart Peddlers* to despair in Albee's *The Zoo Story*.

The phonetic transcription in the *Annotations* is from D. Jones – A. C. Gimson, *Everyman's English Pronouncing Dictionary*, 14th edition.
The following abbreviations are used in the *Annotations:*

| | | | |
|---|---|---|---|
| *A.E.* | American English | *o.s.* | oneself |
| *B.E.* | British English | *s.b.* | somebody |
| *coll.* | colloquial | *s.o.* | someone |
| *sl.* | slang | *s.th.* | something |
| *dial.* | dialect | | |

Numbers in bold-face type in the margin refer to the corresponding pages in the text, those in light-face type to the lines of the respective page. Example: **25** 23 = page 25, line 23.

# A Note to the Teacher

Being well aware of a distinction between a pleasant private indulgence in literature and a critical approach which is based on intellectual appreciation rather than taste, the teacher of literature is confronted with two problems: On the one hand it will be necessary to pave the students' way for pleasurable reading in the future by leaving them as much room as the curriculum allows to ask their own questions, find their own answers, and concentrate on what they consider interesting; on the other hand it will be necessary to introduce critical methods, technical terms, and provide background information, to guide and explain.

Consequently it will always depend on the individual teacher's intention and the ambitions and abilities of the class to what extent the suggestions and analyses in this book are taken into account.

In any case, the selection of one-act plays at hand allows for purely pleasurable reading as well as more academic considerations: The plays are short, the vocabulary is not difficult. Written between 1931 *(The Happy Journey to Trenton and Camden)* and 1980 *(The Pushcart Peddlers),* the plays deal with a society the contemporary reader is well familiar with – a society reeling from events which have called into question the very foundation of modern morality and expectations. Therefore, upon reading and reflection, the student will hopefully come to a fairly clear understanding of the inner nature of American culture in particular and western culture in general.

Furthermore, the plays are full of modern theatrical devices, and thus give ample opportunity to introduce or further explain the theory of modern drama.

And last but not least, the subject matter of all four dramas is of particular interest: Although we cannot consider 20th-century American literature a mere synthesis of local and foreign influences – with national peculiarities and characteristics generally being less prominent in modern literature – the sequence presented here allows the focus on the development of what we refer to as the "American Dream". We have the optimistic "immigrant entrepreneurs" Cornelius and Shimmel in Schisgal's highly amusing play, and Wilder's Ma Kirby who feels safe and sheltered in a happy family, guiding her life under the conviction that "God knows best". On the other hand, there is the aging traveling salesman, a true colleague of Miller's Willy Loman, who notices a deplorable value-shift from "solidity" to "productivity", and Albee's bitter *Zoo Story* which annihilates everything society has recommended as a model or has considered an important value.

Apart from genre questions and character types the first play's analysis focuses on the immigration theme and the clash between illusion and reality on a fictitious as well as an historic level.

Thornton Wilder's play justifies a more formalistic approach as it deliberately makes use of novel dramatic devices such as the Brechtian "alienation effect" (or "A-effect" for short).

In Williams' *The Last of My Solid Gold Watches* the emphasis lies on the protagonist and the values he represents.

Albee's play is the longest and probably most difficult one in this sequence; therefore the analysis first of all tries to help the students reach a general understanding of the play, rather than discuss single prominent aspects of it. The play's affiliation with the Theatre of the Absurd should be discussed with more advanced students only, as it would require comparative literature studies and the reading of theoretical texts.

Generally speaking, we have not attempted to offer the students an interpretation that is not open to dispute. It seems more useful to offer them techniques and perspectives that will develop their interpretive abilities in the long run, and that will allow them to come to their own conclusions beyond what can be generally agreed on.The content and aims of the teaching notes are, however, based on our understanding of the works as described in the section "Content and Analysis". The analyses permit an overall view of the plays' dimensions and, in the case of *The Zoo Story,* the spectrum of academic responses. Grammar and reading exercises or comprehension questions are not provided, as those would largely depend on the individual needs of the class. The section "For Further Study" makes suggestions for comparative reading and additional units.

Three of the four plays (*The Happy Journey to Trenton and Camden* being the exception) were recorded for this publication. The recordings will occasionally be referred to in the analyses. The cassette is not only recommended in order to make it quite clear that a drama is meant to be performed, spoken, acted. It also serves the purpose of creating curiosity and giving pleasure – thus motivating an appreciative as well as intellectual approach.

Murray Schisgal

# The Pushcart Peddlers

Characters:

CORNELIUS J. HOLLINGSWORTH III

SHIMMEL SHITZMAN

MAGGIE CUTWELL

Scene:

*Waterfront, New York City.*

Time:

*Many years ago.*

At Rise:

*A backdrop on which there is painted almost photographic, a symmetrically designed Customs House, side and front view: smaller buildings nearby.*

*Several kegs and wooden crates at both sides of backdrop. Lidded trash-can, downstage.*

*Sound: waterfront noises, steamship whistle.*

*Music: in the style of the Ragtime section of Zukerman/Bolling "Suite for Violin and Jazz Piano."*

*Cornelius, in vest, collarless shirt, baggy pants and a soiled derby, is seated on a wooden box beside his banana-filled pushcart; his legs are crossed and a newspaper is spread in front of his face.*

*Shimmel enters, looks about, and proceeds across stage. He carries a battered suitcase, wears a threadbare suit, open-necked shirt and wilted tie, a soft cap on his head.*

*Music out.*

CORNELIUS *(as Shimmel passes, peeks out from behind newspaper)* Bananas. *(Shimmel stops, turns to Cornelius, waits in vain for him to speak further, then moves on. Cornelius, peeking out from behind newspaper)* Bananas.

SHIMMEL *(stops again)* Excuse me.

CORNELIUS *(rises; folds and puts newspaper on pushcart; expansively)* What a day! What a beautiful day. When I got up this morning I said to myself, "This is going to be one rotten day." But look at it. Look for yourself. It's a beautiful day. Absolutely beautiful. It just goes to show you. You can't be too smart in this world. *(snaps open paper bag)* How many?

SHIMMEL How many what?

CORNELIUS How many bananas do you want?

SHIMMEL I don't want any bananas.

CORNELIUS You don't want any bananas?

SHIMMEL *(shakes his head)* No.

CORNELIUS Then why did you disturb me?

SHIMMEL I thought you were talking to me.

CORNELIUS You thought ...? Why should I talk to you? Are you a millionaire? *(Shimmel shakes his head.)* Are you a politician? *(Shimmel shakes his head.)* Are you a celebrity? *(Shimmel shakes his head.)* Then why should I talk to you?

SHIMMEL I ... I'm sorry, I made a mistake. It is a beautiful day. A wonderful day. Excuse me. *(He starts off.)*

CORNELIUS *(returns paper bag)* The nerve of some people. Coming over and making a spectacle of themselves. Hey, you!

SHIMMEL *(runs to him)* Yes?

CORNELIUS Who are you, anyway?

SHIMMEL *(removes cap, pushes it into jacket pocket)* Shitzman. Shimmel Shitzman.

CORNELIUS *(amazed)* You're Shimmel Shitzman?

SHIMMEL Do you know me?

CORNELIUS Why should I know you? Are you a millionaire? *(Shimmel shakes his head.)* Are you a politician? *(Shimmel shakes his head.)* Are you a celebrity? *(Shimmel shakes his head.)* Then why should I know you?

SHIMMEL I thought you ...

CORNELIUS Where are you from, Shimmel Shitzman?

SHIMMEL From the vicinity of Kovno-Vilna.

CORNELIUS *(amazed)* You're from the vicinity of Kovno-Vilna?

SHIMMEL Are you from the vicinity of Kovno-Vilna?

CORNELIUS *(dusts bananas with feather mop)* As a matter of fact, I'm not. I'm from the vicinity of Minsk-Pinsk.

SHIMMEL *(enthusiastically)* Minsk-Pinsk! Why, that's practically walking distance from the vicinity of Kovno-Vilna. We're practically neighbors!

CORNELIUS Does that surprise you?

SHIMMEL In all honesty, it does. You're the first person I talked to since I got off the boat. And to talk to someone who was practically my neighbor in the old country, that's what I call a stroke of good luck. Can I ask you a few impersonal questions, neighbor?

CORNELIUS *(sits)* So long as you don't take up too much of my time, neighbor. You happen to have caught me during my rush hour.

SHIMMEL Business is good?

CORNELIUS Business is excellent. Couldn't be better.

SHIMMEL When did you arrive from Minsk-Pinsk?

CORNELIUS Is today Tuesday or Wednesday?

SHIMMEL Wednesday.

CORNELIUS Then I arrived yesterday.

SHIMMEL *(puts suitcase down)* You arrived yesterday from Minsk-Pinsk?

CORNELIUS That's correct.

SHIMMEL And you're in business for yourself already?

CORNELIUS That's correct. *(He lights a cigar butt.)*

SHIMMEL Why, that's wonderful, marvelous!

CORNELIUS You think that's wonderful, marvelous? I heard of a man from the vicinity of Ozrokow-Pruszkow who arrived here in the morning and owned two factories, three warehouses and a hotel in the Catskill Mountains before he sat down for lunch!

SHIMMEL Fantastic! What a country this is! What a great country. I can't wait to get started myself, but ...

CORNELIUS But what?

SHIMMEL I don't know where to begin.

CORNELIUS Well, since we're practically from the same vicinity ... maybe I can give you a hint or two.

SHIMMEL *(sits on suitcase)* I would appreciate that more than anything in the world.

CORNELIUS *(with emphasis)* Are you listening?

SHIMMEL I'm listening.

CORNELIUS Are you paying attention?

SHIMMEL I'm paying attention.

CORNELIUS First thing you have to do ...

SHIMMEL Yes?

CORNELIUS Is buy yourself an American name.

SHIMMEL Buy myself an American name?

CORNELIUS That's absolutely essential, *(steps on cigar butt; takes slips of papers from vest pocket.)* And I'll tell you something else, neighbor: this is your lucky day. It so happens I have several American names that are up for sale.

SHIMMEL But what's wrong with Shimmel Shitzman?

CORNELIUS Shimmel Shitzman? They'll laugh you out of the country with a name like that. Do you know what my name was when I got off the boat? *(Shimmel shakes his head.)* Elias Crapavarnishkes.

SHIMMEL Crapavarnishkes. That's not a bad name. There was a judge from the vicinity of Lvov who had the name Crapavarnishkes. He was a very respected man.

CORNELIUS Your Judge Crapavarnishkes couldn't get a job as a street cleaner here. The first thing I did when I got off the boat was to buy myself a brand new legitimate name. And since then I've been prospering beyond my wildest dreams.

SHIMMEL That's fantastic. What is your American name?

CORNELIUS *(slight English accent)* Cornelius J. Hollingsworth.

SHIMMEL Wow!

CORNELIUS The Third.

SHIMMEL The Third?

CORNELIUS That's correct. It cost me fifteen dollars with the middle initial and the Third thrown in. It was the only one like it they had. I could have gotten John Smith for fifty cents, but I wouldn't have any part of it. Well, what do you say, Mr. Shitzman? *(Reading from slips of paper.)* I have Andrew Hamilton for five dollars, Sylvester Peterson for six-fifty, Thomas Hathaway, six dollars and fifteen cents, Roger Williams Carnegie, five seventy-five, Samuel P. Stone, five dollars without the tax ...

SHIMMEL I'm sorry, Mr. Hollingsworth. I couldn't change my name. It's been in my family for generations. I was born a Shitzman and I guess I'll have to die a Shitzman.

CORNELIUS *(returning slips of paper to vest pocket)* Have it your own way. But don't say I didn't try to help you. It just goes to show: mind your own business and you're better off. *(Indignantly, he spreads newspaper in front of his face.)*

SHIMMEL *(rises; lifts suitcase)* Mr. Hollingsworth?

CORNELIUS *(behind newspaper)* What is it now?

SHIMMEL Can I ask you one more question?

CORNELIUS *(behind newspaper)* I told you I was busy! I don't have all day to sit here and chat with you!

SHIMMEL One more question and I won't bother you any more, I promise.

CORNELIUS *(puts newspaper aside)* Go on. What is it? What is it?

SHIMMEL *(puts suitcase down)* Where do you think I should look for a job?

CORNELIUS A job? Why do you want to look for a job?

SHIMMEL To work. To earn money ...

CORNELIUS Ridiculous. Nobody comes to this country to look for a job. There's no future in it. You have to go into business for yourself. It's the only decent way to make a living here.

SHIMMEL *(sits on suitcase)* But I don't know anything about going into business. I'm a worker. I have experience as a tinsmith, a carpenter, a ...

CORNELIUS You people from the vicinity of Kovno-Vilna are all a bunch of blockheads! What did I know about going into business when I got off the boat? Nothing. Absolutely nothing. I was a shoemaker, a leather-stitcher. But did I let that stop me? Not on your life. I used my head and here I am: in business for myself!

SHIMMEL But what kind of business could I get into? I don't have much capital ...

CORNELIUS Ohhh, there are plenty of good profitable businesses you can go into. Why don't you open your eyes and look around and see what's available? *(As Shimmel rises and "looks around," Cornelius plants a FOR SALE on his pushcart.)* If I were you, Mr. Shitzman, I'd grab the first business up for sale and get right to work. I wouldn't waste any time. Things happen fast in this country. Very fast. You have to stay up on your toes and use your old noodle! *(He spreads newspaper in front of his face.)*

SHIMMEL *(turns to see sign on pushcart)* Mr. Hollingsworth?

CORNELIUS *(behind newspaper)* Yes?

SHIMMEL Is your ... business up for sale?

CORNELIUS *(folds newspaper; stares at FOR SALE sign)* Hmmmmmm. As a matter of fact, it is.

SHIMMEL Do you think I could make a go of it?

CORNELIUS *(puts newspaper aside; rises)* You?

SHIMMEL *(nods)* Me.

CORNELIUS Hmmmmmm. That's a *tough* question. Let me hear you say: bananas.

SHIMMEL Bananas.

CORNELIUS Hmmmmmm. You're not without talent. Let me hear you say: bananas, bananas, get your fresh ripe bananas!

SHIMMEL Bananas, bananas, get your fresh ripe bananas!

CORNELIUS Try it a little louder and try to speak out of the side of your mouth so your voice has a distinctive quality: bananas, bananas, get your fresh ripe bananas!

SHIMMEL *(imitating him: from the side of his mouth, jerking his head)* Bananas, bananas, get your fresh ripe bananas!

CORNELIUS No, no, your arms have to swing out, from the side, as if you own the whole street. And kick your leg up a little. Like this. *(demonstrating: throws arms out, kicks up one leg, tips derby on last word)* Bananas, bananas, get your fresh ripe bananas! *(to Shimmel)* Try it. *(He puts derby on Shimmel's head; sits on trash can.)*

SHIMMEL *(imitating him)* Bananas, bananas, get your fresh ripe bananas! *(tips derby)*

CORNELIUS Excellent. Excellent. How did it feel?

SHIMMEL Fine. It felt fine.

CORNELIUS Were you relaxed? Were you comfortable?

SHIMMEL I was very relaxed and comfortable.

CORNELIUS *(rises)* I'm going to tell you something now, Mr. Shitzman: between the two of us and the pushcart, you'll make a fortune in this business.

SHIMMEL *(excitedly)* You think so?

CORNELIUS *(takes derby from Shimmel's head; puts it on)* I know so. It's a definite positive.

SHIMMEL How much would it cost me?

CORNELIUS *(moves to pushcart; arms outspread)* The whooole business?

SHIMMEL *(nods)* The whole business.

CORNELIUS Hmmmmmm. I could ... no, no, I couldn't do that. We're practically from the same vicinity. Let me ask you this, Mr. Shitzman. How much do you have?

SHIMMEL I have exactly ... *(takes out change purse)* Forty-three dollars and twenty-five cents.

CORNELIUS Could you raise another six dollars and seventy-five cents by five o'clock?

SHIMMEL *(sits on trash can)* How? I don't know anyone here.

CORNELIUS *(sits on box)* What a shame! I couldn't possibly sell for under fifty dollars unless ... *(rises)*

SHIMMEL *(rises)* Unless what?

CORNELIUS Unless I took a bunch of bananas to make up the difference.

SHIMMEL A bunch of bananas is worth six dollars and seventy-five cents?

CORNELIUS *(He picks up a bunch of bananas.)* Are you serious? Do you know what they call a bunch of bananas in this country? *(Shimmel shakes his head. Cornelius holds out bananas, pointed upwards.)* Goldfingers.

SHIMMEL That's fantastic! Here you are, Mr. Hollingsworth. *(gives him money)* I'm anxious to get right to work. Do I need any papers to prove ownership?

CORNELIUS *(bananas under arm)* You'll find them under the fifth banana in the fourth row from the left. *(shakes his hand)* Congratulations Mr. Shitzman. And the best of everything to you.

SHIMMEL Thank you. Thank you, Mr. Hollingsworth.

CORNELIUS *(moving off)* I have to be off now. If you sell out, go to Pier 26 and ask for Pete. He'll give you a fair shake.

SHIMMEL *(shouts after him)* Thanks again, Mr. Hollingsworth. And drop around and say hello once in a while! *(Music. Shimmel puts on cap, carries suitcase behind pushcart, places FOR SALE sign on top of it; he then examines pushcart, proudly, with proprietary air; he dusts off bananas with feather mop, dusts off his jacket, looks about as if he owns the whole street. He suddenly shouts, swinging his arms, kicks up a leg, in imitation of Cornelius.)* Bananas, bananas, get your fresh ripe bananas! *(He runs to pushcart, snaps open a paper bag, as if expecting an avalanche of customers. Undismayed he returns paper bag, sits on box, crossing his legs, and spreads the newspaper in front of his face. Offstage Cornelius shouts, "Bananas, bananas, get your fresh ripe bananas!" Shimmel lowers his newspaper and gapes in astonishment as Cornelius rolls in a second pushcart, an exact replica of the one he sold to him, shouting, two or three times more, "Bananas, bananas, get your fresh ripe bananas!" Cornelius stops his pushcart parallel to Shimmel's, removes a wooden box from it, sits down and unfolds a newspaper in front of his face. Music out. Shimmel removes his cap, speaks softly, uncertainly.)* Mr. Hollingsworth?

CORNELIUS *(behind newspaper)* Yes?

SHIMMEL You're not staying here, are you?

CORNELIUS *(behind newspaper)* Of course I'm staying here. *(reads aloud)* Hmmmmmm. This is interesting. "Bride hurls wedding cake at groom for criticizing her dress. Brawl ensues." *(He hawks a laugh.)*

SHIMMEL But ...

CORNELIUS But what?

SHIMMEL But can we both make a living selling the same merchandise at the same location?

CORNELIUS *(puts newspaper aside; rises)* Unfortunately we can't. The competition will force us to lower the price and we'll probably have to begin bankruptcy proceedings in a matter of days. *(shouts)* Bananas, bananas!

SHIMMEL *(rises; desperately)* Mr. Hollingsworth!

CORNELIUS What is it now?

SHIMMEL I don't want to sound rude, but if we both can't make a living here, why don't you be considerate and go somewhere else?

CORNELIUS Why don't I ... *(sharply)* Why don't you be considerate and go somewhere else?

SHIMMEL It was my understanding when you sold me this business that I would be the only one at this location. Otherwise I can assure you, I would have thought twice about buying it!

CORNELIUS Ohhh, it was your understanding! But I didn't say anything to that effect, did I?

SHIMMEL You didn't have to ...

CORNELIUS This is a free country, Mr. Shitzman, and I have as much right to sell at this location as you have! *(shouts)* Bananas, bananas!

SHIMMEL Can't we talk about it? *(shouts in a panic)* Bananas, bananas!

CORNELIUS Talk, who's stopping you? *(shouts)* Bananas, bananas!

SHIMMEL I'm new here, Mr. Hollingsworth. I don't know this city! *(shouts)* Bananas, bananas!

CORNELIUS Mr. Shitzman, I have to make a living, too. My customers expect to find me here and I'm not disappointing them! Not for you or the King of Siam! *(shouts)* Bananas, bananas!

SHIMMEL Mr. Hollingsworth, I gave you my last penny! I trusted you! *(shouts)* Bananas, bananas!

CORNELIUS I can't help you more than I did, Mr. Shitzman! *(shouts)* Bananas! Bana ... *(Suddenly turns to Shimmel.)* Unless ...

SHIMMEL *(eagerly)* Unless what?

CORNELIUS Unless we went into partnership.

SHIMMEL Partnership?

CORNELIUS *(nods)* The two of us.

SHIMMEL Why, that would be wonderful, Mr. ...

CORNELIUS *(grins)* Call me Cornelius.

SHIMMEL Cornelius. Cornelius, that would be wonderful! It would solve all our problems! We could work together, cooperate ...

CORNELIUS There's only one thing that stands in the way.

SHIMMEL What's that?

CORNELIUS *(sits on trash can)* Money.

SHIMMEL Money?

CORNELIUS That's correct. Money. You don't expect us to become full and equal partners with all my experience, do you?

SHIMMEL But I don't have any money left, Mr. ... Cornelius. I gave you my last penny, word of honor. *(He raises his hand.)*

CORNELIUS Can't you borrow some from friends or relatives or a philanthropic organization?

SHIMMEL *(sits on box)* Impossible. I told you, I don't know anyone here.

CORNELIUS *(rises)* Then there's only one thing for us to do.

SHIMMEL *(rises)* What's that?

CORNELIUS Negotiate.

SHIMMEL Can we negotiate without money?

CORNELIUS Of course.

SHIMMEL How do we do it?

CORNELIUS *(using his hands)* It's simple. You make an offer. I refuse your offer and make a counter-offer. You refuse my counter-offer and make a counter-counter-offer of your own. I refuse your counter-counter-offer and I make what is called a proposal which leads you to make a counter-proposal and so on and so forth and so on and so forth until we whittle the difference to nil and come to equitable terms.

SHIMMEL But I still don't have any money.

CORNELIUS Who's talking about money! Jesus Christ, you are a dumb-dumb. We negotiate percentages! *(Throws arms out at one pushcart, then the other.)* How much of the business do you own in contradistinction to how much of the business do I own! *(He sits on box, crosses legs, puts newspaper in front of his face.)* Make me an offer.

SHIMMEL On a percentage of the business?

CORNELIUS *(behind newspaper)* That's correct. Do it formally.

SHIMMEL Yes, sir. *(Puts on cap, brushes jacket; clears throat.)* Excuse me, Mr. Hollingsworth.

CORNELIUS *(newspaper on lap; innocently)* Did you wish to speak to me, sir?

SHIMMEL Yes, sir. About the possibility of our going into partnership, sir. I make an offer that you receive fifty percent of the business and I receive fifty percent of the business ... sir.

CORNELIUS What about my superior experience, sir?

SHIMMEL I can learn the business very quickly and if I work twice as hard that will offset the difference, sir.

CORNELIUS No deal, sir. I respectfully decline your offer. *(Newspaper in front of his face.)*

SHIMMEL *(clears throat; whispers)* You make your counter-offer now. *(no response)* I make my offer, fifty-fifty, you're supposed to make a counter-offer. *(no response; loudly)* Aren't you going to make me a counter-offer, sir? Did I do anything improper, sir? *(desperately)* Mr. Hollingsworth, we have to reach an agreement! You yourself said we both can't make a living here! For God's sake, make me a counter-offer!

CORNELIUS *(lowers newspaper)* Bananas, ripe lovely bananas here! *(Newspaper in front of his face.)*

SHIMMEL This is crazy! You're being unfair, unreasonable! I ... *(resigned to it)* All right, sixty-forty! Sixty for you, forty for me. Is it a deal sir?

CORNELIUS *(puts newspaper aside: shouts)* Bananas, get your ripe lovely bananas here! *(without looking at him; coaching him)* Get down on your knees. Beg me. Tell me how hard up you are. Tell me your family depends on you for support. Get to me emotionally. *(shouts)* Bananas, bananas here! Get your ripe bananas!

SHIMMEL *(on his knees)* Mr. Hollingsworth, I beg you to consider my offer. I think it's very equitable. Besides, I'm broke. I don't have a penny. I don't have money to buy dinner tonight ... I don't have a roof over my head ... *(Cornelius rises, paces. Shimmel is emotional indeed, on the verge of tears, building his lines to a crescendo.)* Mr. Hollingsworth, my family is still in the old country. They're depending on me to send them something each week. I have an elderly father who's confined to his bed. My mother suffers from arthritis and bursitis. My two little sisters don't have clothes to wear to school. My baby brother, my little baby brother ... *(He breaks into sobs.)*

CORNELIUS *(tears streaming down his cheeks)* What a terrible story. What a tragedy. How old is your little baby brother?

SHIMMEL *(weeping)* Who knows? Who knows?

CORNELIUS *(weeping)* What dis-ease, what afflic-tion does he have?

SHIMMEL *(weeping; louder)* Who knows? Who knows?

CORNELIUS *(weeping)* Your two little sisters ...

SHIMMEL *(weeping; still louder)* My two little sisters ... without clothes!

CORNELIUS *(weeping)* Don't say another word, Shimmel. Please, please don't! Not another word! I'll help you. I'll do whatever you want.

SHIMMEL *(rises)* Does that mean we're partners?

CORNELIUS Sixty-forty?

SHIMMEL *(nods)* Sixty-forty!

CORNELIUS *(embracing him)* Partner!

SHIMMEL Thank you, Cornelius; thank you.

CORNELIUS *(breaks away, takes out handkerchief, blows his nose)* Oh, boy, that was a good cry. Oh, boy. I have to admit ... I enjoyed it thoroughly.

SHIMMEL *(wiping his eyes)* I did, too. I didn't know that negotiations could be so emotional.

CORNELIUS There's a lot you have to learn, partner. But don't worry. I'll teach you every aspect of this business. From now on your gain becomes under contract my profit. Okay, now let's get to work. No more horsing around.

*(Music. Cornelius sits down on box, crosses legs, spreads newspaper in front of his face. Shimmel, imitating him, does likewise. Cornelius soon rises, yawns, stretches his arms over his head, shakes out one leg, then the other, looks about, then flaps handkerchief over top of wooden box before sitting down, spreading newspaper in front of his face. Shimmel does likewise, but before spreading newspaper in front of his face, speaks. Music out.)*

SHIMMEL Cornelius?

CORNELIUS *(behind newspaper)* Yes?

SHIMMEL How's business?

CORNELIUS *(newspaper on lap)* Excellent. Excellent. If it keeps up at this rate, I think we should buy another pushcart.

SHIMMEL Can we afford it?

CORNELIUS What a question.

SHIMMEL I didn't know we were that successful.

CORNELIUS If I told you how successful we were, Shimmel, you'd get a swollen head, so let's not discuss it and just keep working.

SHIMMEL I will. I promise. You'll get nothing but hard work from me.

CORNELIUS That's what I expect from you. Now let's get to work.

*(They both spread their newspapers in front of their faces. Romantic, lyrical music. Maggie Cutwell, a young, very pretty girl, in a shapeless black frock, enters, carrying a tray of small bunches of colorful flowers strapped around her neck. She walks with her hand held* slightly *in front of her.)*

MAGGIE *(in a sweet, angelic voice)* Flowers. Flowers. Pretty flowers for sale. Fresh, pretty flowers. *(She doesn't turn to the men but stands at the side of Shimmel's pushcart, staring forward. She wipes her perspiring face with a rag. Music out.)*

SHIMMEL *(whispers; puts newspaper aside)* Cornelius? Do you see that?

CORNELIUS *(puts newspaper aside)* Oh, yes.

SHIMMEL She's beautiful, isn't she?

CORNELIUS I've seen better heads on cabbages. But it's a pity, just the same.

SHIMMEL What's a pity?

CORNELIUS She's blind.

SHIMMEL Is she?

CORNELIUS All the flower girls are blind in this country.

SHIMMEL That is a pity. She looks destitute. She looks like she hasn't had a piece of food in her mouth all day. Cornelius, can I get a credit for one banana?

CORNELIUS *(makes an entry in notebook)* If you want to be extravagant ...

SHIMMEL Thank you. *(He takes banana from pushcart and moves to Maggie. She doesn't turn to look at him. Gently he places the banana on her flower tray; returns to his seat.)*

MAGGIE *(looks down at banana; shouts)* Get your fucking banana off my fucking flowers!

SHIMMEL *(jumps up, retrieves banana)* Forgive me. I ... I thought you were blind.

MAGGIE I'll give you blind in a minute. I'll poke out both your eyes and feed 'em to the cats!

SHIMMEL But I ...

MAGGIE I know what you're after, Buster! If I wanted to be a whore, I wouldn't be selling these fucking flowers!

SHIMMEL You're mistaken, believe me. I only wanted to help you.

MAGGIE Yeah, and how the hell were you gonna do that? By slipping me a banana?

SHIMMEL I thought you were hungry.

MAGGIE I don't need your lousy banana. If I'm hungry, I know where to eat. I've been taking care of myself since I'm six years old and I haven't starved to death yet!

SHIMMEL You're an orphan?

MAGGIE You bet your sweet ass!

SHIMMEL I'm sorry. Life must have been difficult for you.

MAGGIE I got no complaints. How about buying a bunch of these stinkweeds for your girl friend?

SHIMMEL I'm afraid I have no money. *(laughs self-consciously)* I have no girl friend either.

MAGGIE That figures, you crumb-bum, you creep! Wasting a girl's time for nothing. I oughta call the police. I oughta bop you in the nose. *(Shouts as she forces him back so that he sits on trash can.)* Get away from me! I hate your lousy guts! *(Suddenly in a sweet, angelic voice.)* Flowers. Pretty flowers for sale. Fresh pretty flowers. *(Cornelius rises, derby in hand; he moves to Maggie, speaks with great formality.)*

CORNELIUS Allow me to apologize for my partner, ma'am. He's new here. He has no sense of propriety.

MAGGIE They should send him back where he came from, the creep! Doesn't he have the decency to introduce himself like a gentleman? Did his parents name him before they dumped him into a garbage can?

CORNELIUS His name is Shitzman. Shimmel Shitzman.

*(Shimmel stands as if expecting an introduction.)*

MAGGIE Shitzman! Shimmel Shitzman! *(She breaks out into laughter.)* It fits him. It fits him perfectly. *(to Shimmel)* Shitzman. Mr. Shitzman! *(And she laughs again.)*

*(Shimmel sits down on trash can, dejectedly.)*

CORNELIUS *(bows)* Perhaps you'd be good enough to permit me to introduce myself to you, ma'am. I am Cornelius J. Hollingsworth, the Third.

MAGGIE *(curtsies a bit)* Pleased to make your acquaintance, Mr. Hollingsworth. I am Maggie Cutwell and although I find it necessary to sell flowers in order to sustain myself, I am by profession an actress, a thespian, a tap dancer, a toe dancer, and a highly regarded chanteuse.

CORNELIUS All good fortune to you, Miss Cutwell. I am myself in the banana business at present, but it is merely transitional. My one true and genuine ambition is to gain a seat on the Stock Exchange and invest substantial sums of money in musical comedy productions. *(Puts on derby.)*

MAGGIE Am I to believe that it is your intention to become a theatrical producer?

CORNELIUS Precisely, Miss Cutwell. *(picks up a banana)* May I offer you a banana?

MAGGIE *(takes it from him)* I will be happy to take your banana, Mr. Hollingsworth, but I will never take his banana. *(to Shimmel)* Never! Not even if it was covered with diamonds!

CORNELIUS I am doing all I can for him, Miss Cutwell, but it's a sad, a terribly sad and tragic story.

MAGGIE I'm sure it is.

CORNELIUS How much are your flowers, Miss Cutwell?

MAGGIE These are ten cents a bunch, and those wilted ones on the side are three cents a bunch.

CORNELIUS I would like to purchase two ten cent bunches, please. *(She hands them to him; he gives her the coins.)* Thank you. Here's your money and these ... these are for you. *(Gallantly he hands her back the flowers. He then passes Shimmel, extending his arms as if to say, "See how easy it is?")*

MAGGIE You are a very kind person, I can see that right away. Mr. Hollingsworth, it may be premature of me to suggest, but in the event you actually become a theatrical producer in the foreseeable future, could you possibly keep me in mind for a part in one of your musical productions?

CORNELIUS To be frank with you, Miss Cutwell, I don't know whether you're talented or not.

MAGGIE Can't I show you? Won't you at least give me the opportunity to show you what I can do?

CORNELIUS Ordinarily I would say yes immediately, without reservation, but you've caught me during my busiest day of the week. It's impossible. I can't. I have obligations. *(He puts foot on box, ties his shoelace.)*

MAGGIE Please, Mr. Hollingsworth! This is extremely important to me. If I don't succeed in my chosen profession, I'll have to go on selling flowers for the rest of my life, or marry some beer-bellied creep who'd beat me every night just for the exercise. I'll be forced to kill myself, Mr. Hollingsworth! *(Cornelius turns to her as she gets down on her knees.)* I couldn't go on living like that, I couldn't, I couldn't ... *(She weeps.)*

CORNELIUS *(tears streaming down his cheeks)* What a tragedy. What a terrible, terrible story. How long have you been selling flowers?

MAGGIE *(weeping)* Ever since I was six years old.

CORNELIUS *(weeping)* Tragic. Tragic. Have you experienced no pleasure, no happiness, no joy in all your young years?

MAGGIE *(weeping)* No. Nothing but pain and heartache.

CORNELIUS *(weeping)* Ohhhhh, pain and heartache. And you would take your own life?

MAGGIE *(weeping)* Yes, yes, I have the pills at home and today there was a sale at Woolworth's and I bought ... I bought six bottles of iodine!

CORNELIUS *(moves away; she follows him on her knees)* No more, Miss Cutwell. No more. I can't take it. I can't. It's too much for a human being to bear. If you'd like to perform for me, go home, change, rearrange your appearance, prepare yourself, and come back when you're ready. But please, hurry. I don't have the time! I have a business to run here!

MAGGIE Thank you. Thank you. You're my light in the darkness. You're my savior. *(rises)* Two minutes, Mr. Hollingsworth. *(turns to Shimmel)* Two minutes ... Sh-Sh-Sh-Sh-Shitzman? Shitzman? That's a riot. Shitzman. *(And she exits.)*

CORNELIUS *(sits on box)* Well, what do you think?

SHIMMEL *(rises; looks after Maggie)* I ... I think she's beautiful.

CORNELIUS Good. I'm glad you feel that way because I'd like you to get her off my hands.

SHIMMEL But I thought ...

CORNELIUS *(rises; moves to him)* Don't think, Shimmel. You can be arrested for it. Feel, feel, start feeling and start expressing your feelings, your fantasies, your dreams! Use your imagination! You're a very repressed person. If I had known that before, I would never have gone into partnership with you!

**SHIMMEL** But why do you want me to take Miss Cutwell off your hands? Aren't you attracted to her?

**CORNELIUS** Attracted, retracted, contracted, who has time for those shenanigans. It so happens, be it as it may, willy-nilly, hocus-pocus, I'm a married man. *(moves toward his box; stops)* I also have three brats. *(moves; stops)* And a gypsy girl friend. *(moves)* It's unprofessional for me to get further involved. *(Sits on box.)*

**SHIMMEL** I'd be very glad to take her off your hands.

**CORNELIUS** Excellent. Excellent. *(rises)* Unfortunately one problem remains.

**SHIMMEL** What's that?

**CORNELIUS** Our partnership name. Hollingsworth and Shitzman. It's out of the question. Didn't you hear how Miss Cutwell laughed at it? We'll get the same treatment from everyone who hears it. We'll be the laughing stock of the banana business.

**SHIMMEL** But I told you ...

**CORNELIUS** *(shouts)* I know what you told me! I know what you said! But don't I count for anything? Shimmel, please! Consider someone else for a change? There's no limit to how far we could go together, but you're destroying everything we created with your ridiculous name! It's like a cancer preventing our full growth and prosperity!

**SHIMMEL** Even if I wanted to ... I don't have the money ...

**CORNELIUS** *(sits on box)* We'll negotiate. I'll take an I.O.U. I'll place a lien on your forty percent. Don't worry about it. *(pulls out slips of paper)* Now what will it be? Thomas Hathaway. Roger Williams Carnegie. Samuel P. Stone ...

**SHIMMEL** *(pleading)* Cornelius, my family name ... *(sits on box)*

**CORNELIUS** Which one, Shimmel? Which one? *(Shimmel doesn't reply. Cornelius rises; hands him slip of paper.)* Samuel P. Stone it is! Five dollars even. Hollingsworth and Stone. Perfect. It couldn't be better. Congratulations, partner. *(sits; makes entry in notebook)* Well, do you feel any differently, Sam? *(Shimmel shakes his head.)* You have to feel differently. A Crapavarnishkes isn't a Hollingsworth and a Shitzman isn't a Stone.

**SHIMMEL** Samuel P. Stone. I am Samuel P. Stone.

**CORNELIUS** Sam Stone!

SHIMMEL *(rises)* I am Sam Stone. *(He faces upstage.)*

CORNELIUS That's it. Feel Stone. Feel rock. Feel hard. Feel firm. Feel strong. Feel ...

*(Maggie rushes back in, wearing a Shirley Temple dress and tap shoes.)*

MAGGIE *(panting)* I'm here, Mr. Hollingsworth! I'm ready to perform for you.

CORNELIUS *(rises)* Yes, yes, but before you begin, I'd like to introduce you to my partner, Sam Stone.

MAGGIE But that's Mr. Shitzman. I met him ...

CORNELIUS I beg to differ with you, Miss Cutwell. That *was* Mr. Shitzman. But he has changed considerably since you last saw him.

*(Shimmel turns downstage, posture straight, hand in pocket; speaks with pronounced certainty and sophistication.)*

SHIMMEL That's correct, Miss Cutwell. And if you've come to perform for us, please begin. We don't have all day to dilly-dally.

*(Both men nod to each other, curtly, and return to sit on their boxes. Maggie looks about to make sure no one is about, then breaks into a bright song and tap dance, something in the style of "I Don't Care." She sings intro without moving, merely bouncing up and down, hands clenched as if riding a horse. She tap dances as she sings the chorus, moving around the peddlers, posing beside them – a nightclub performance of sorts. This is followed by a tap dance as she da-da's tune of chorus. She ends by whirling around several times, almost stumbling. Her talent is not noteworthy. When she is done, she turns to them, waits breathlessly for their verdict.)*

CORNELIUS Sam?

SHIMMEL Yes, Cornelius?

CORNELIUS What do you think of her performance?

SHIMMEL *(rises; fervently)* What do I think? Do you have to ask? Are you blind? Are you deaf? Do you not have a heart to feel with? I have just witnessed a performance of such precision, of such exquisiteness and beauty, that if I were in the producing business today, this young lady would be a star tomorrow!

MAGGIE *(embracing him)* Oh, Mr. Stone! You don't know how much I needed to hear that! You made me so happy!

SHIMMEL *(circling around her)* Enough of this, enough! You have a lot of work to do, Maggie. I am not now in the producing business, but I have every hope of being in the producing business in the very near future. Go home and practice! Practice! Practice! Day and night! Twenty-four hours around the clock! I'm going to be relentless with you, I give you fair warning. I'll pay the bills; I'll see to it that you have the necessities ... *(stops circling; holds her chin in his hand)* But I want you to be the best there is, the absolute best!

MAGGIE I will be! I will! *(Starts off.)*

SHIMMEL And Maggie ...

MAGGIE *(returns)* Yes, Mr. Stone?

SHIMMEL No intimacy. No personal relationship. This is strictly a professional deal, is that clear?

MAGGIE Yes, Mr. Stone. *(Starts off.)*

SHIMMEL Where did you say you lived?

MAGGIE *(returns)* Number eleven Perry Street.

SHIMMEL I'll be up this evening to formalize our contractual arrangement.

MAGGIE I'll be home. I'll be practicing.

SHIMMEL Have a bite for me to eat. I'll be hungry and tired.

MAGGIE I'll put a tuna fish casserole in the oven. Thank you. Thank you, Mr. Stone. I have hope. You gave me hope. God bless you! *(She kisses him on cheek, runs off, singing a line or two of song ending with "2, 3, 4!")*

SHIMMEL *(staring after her)* What a girl! What an incredible girl!

CORNELIUS So you've become fond of her.

SHIMMEL Fond of her? I'm in love with her! I'm head-over-heels in love with her! Cornelius, Cornelius, I never felt this way before. I never thought I could feel this way. My heart is in my mouth. I have a temperature of over a hundred. My legs are shaking. My stomach is bubbling. It's too much. I can't breathe. Is all this happening to me or am I dreaming? Did I meet someone named Maggie Cutwell or did I make it up? Pinch me, Cornelius, pinch me! I have to know the truth!

CORNELIUS *(rises)* Hold it, Sam, just hold it a minute! I have to ask you: are you rich enough to support yourself and her, too? After all, you just started in business, this is your first day here ... I don't unterstand. How can you ...

SHIMMEL You don't understand! Of course you don't understand! You don't look, you don't listen, you don't pay attention! I met a woman I love, Cornelius. I'm going to marry her. She is going to appear in a musical that I am going to produce ... *(points)* with you! Now I have the inspiration, the dedication to succeed in a big way. Nothing can stop me. Nothing! Now, come, no more horsing around. This is a matter of life and death to me. Let's get to work *(He sits on box, crosses legs, puts newspaper in front of his face.)*

CORNELIUS *(stares at him, incredulously; then sits on box, takes newspaper)* How's business, Sam?

SHIMMEL *(behind newspaper)* Good, Cornelius. Excellent.

CORNELIUS You know, I think it's time we started a corporation. What do you think?

SHIMMEL *(newspaper down)* I don't know why we waited so long.

CORNELIUS If I have one fault, it's being too conservative. *(Shimmel puts newspaper in front of his face.)*

CORNELIUS Sam?

SHIMMEL *(newspaper down)* Yes, Cornelius?

CORNELIUS *(simply)* Welcome to America. *(Music as they both lift newspapers in front of their faces, simultaneously uncross and cross their legs – left over right, then right over left – with music punctuating their actions and ending abruptly. Blackout)*

## Biographical Notes

*Murray Schisgal, the son of an immigrant from Vilna, Lithuania, was born in 1929. He has been a New Yorker since birth. He became a serious writer in his late teens, but it was about a decade before he became known.*

*Schisgal, who is a member of the American avant-garde, often takes as his subject the superficiality of modern civilization. He has managed to survive the rise and fall of absurdism by mocking the elements of self-love, self-pity and self-dramatization which often characterize the pessimistic works of many contemporary writers of this mode.*

*In his play entitled "Luv" he satirizes the dishonest way in which many people experience love. This play was extremely well received.*

*Schisgal often uses comedy to get at his serious statements. The humor of "The Pushcart Peddlers" (1980) is an excellent example of his genius in this vein.*

*Among his well-known works are "The Typists" and "The Tiger" (both of which started his career as a dramatist in 1960), "Luv" (1963), "The Old Jew" (1965), "Jimmy Shine" (1969) and "The Chinese" (1970). Several of his plays have been made into films, and he has won various awards. "The Pushcart Peddlers" was published in "The Best Short Plays", 1981.*

## Annotations

**5** **pushcart peddlers** men who move about selling small quantities of goods from two-wheeled vehicles which they push – 10 **backdrop** *Hintergrund-vorhang* – 13 **keg** small barrel – **crate** box for transporting goods – 16 **ragtime** popular music of black American origin – 18 **baggy** hanging loosely – **soiled derby** dirty bowler (hat) – 22 **battered** in poor condition due to hard usage – **threadbare** ['θredbɛə] worn thin; shabby – **wilted** no longer fresh (said usually of plants) – 25 **to peek** to take a short, quick look, often secretly – 30 **expansive** [ɪks'pænsɪv] not holding back

**6** 1 **rotten** *(sl.)* bad – 3 **to snap s.th. open** to open s.th. (like a bag) with a quick turn of the wrist – 14 **celebrity** [sɪ'lebrɪtɪ] s.o. famous – 18 **the nerve of some people** *(coll.)* some people don't know the limits of proper behavior – 19 **to make a spectacle of o.s.** to draw attention to o.s. by behaving ridiculously – 32 **vicinity** [vɪ'sɪnɪtɪ] *nähere Umgebung* – 35 **mop** s.th. with which to dust, usually made out of cloth or feathers

**7** 1 **to get off the boat** (from Europe); "just off the boat" (figurative expression): completely new to America – 2 **a stroke of good luck** [strəʊk] an unexpected happy event – 15 **cigar butt** [sɪ'gɑ:ˌbʌt] last remains of a cigar – 16 **marvelous** ['mɑ:vələs] astonishing; wonderful – 19 **Catskill Mountains** low range of mountains northwest of New York City; favorite vacationing area of New York Jews early in this century – 27 **I would appreciate that** [ə'pri:ʃɪeɪt] I would like that very much

**8** 10 **brand new** absolutely new – **legitimate** lawful; reasonable – **to prosper** to be successful – 17 **initial** (= initial letter) [ɪ'nɪʃl] first letter of a word, a name – 28 **it goes to show** it proves – 29 **indignant** [ɪn'dɪgnənt] angry and scornful – 35 **to chat** to talk with s.o. about unimportant things

**9** 3 **decent** ['di:snt] respectable; *(coll.)* satisfactory, good – 5 **tinsmith** *Klempner* – **carpenter** person who works with wood – 7 **blockhead** ['blɒkhed] *(sl.)* slow and stupid person – 16 **to grab** to take quickly – 19 **to use the old noodle** *(sl.)* (referring to the brain:) to be inventive, clever – 26 **to make a go of s.th.** *(coll.)* to be successful at s.th. – 36 **distinctive** [–'––] special – 38 **to jerk** to move suddenly, quickly

**10** 2 **to tip** (a hat:) to lift a hat slightly off the head in a gesture of politeness – 12 **to make a fortune** to become rich

**11** 6 **to give s.o. a fair shake** *(sl.)* to give s.o. a good financial deal – 10 **proprietary** [–'–––] like an owner – 14 **avalanche** ['–––] *Lawine* – 15 **undismayed** undiscouraged – 18 **to gape** to stare open-mouthed and in surprise – 19 **replica** ['–––] copy – 27 **to hurl** to throw with great energy – 28 **groom** man who is getting married – **brawl ensues** [brɔ:l] fight follows – **to**

**hawk** to hawk a laugh: *here* to laugh from the throat – 31 **merchandise** goods to be sold – 35 **bankruptcy proceedings** ['bænkrəptsı prə'si:dıŋz] legal procedure for going out of business – 40 **(to be) considerate** [kən'sıdərət] to respect s.o. else's needs and desires

**12** 4 **location** [lə'keıʃn] place

**13** 3 **to negotiate** to talk things over in a formal way – 11 **to whittle** ['wıtl] to reduce by degrees – 12 **nil** nothing – **equitable** ['ekwıtəbl] fair, just – 16 **in contradistinction to** (extremely formal) as opposed to

**14** 4 **to coach s.o.** to help s.o. – 5 **to be hard up** *(coll.)* in a bad situation for financial reasons – 9 **broke** *(sl.)* out of money – 11 **to pace** to walk with slow, regular steps (usually back and forth) – 12 **on the verge of** very close to – 13 **the old country** that part of Europe from which o.s. or one's ancestors came – 14 **elderly** ['eldəlı] rather old – **to be confined to (one's bed)** to be unable to leave (one's bed) – 15 **bursitis** [bə'saıtıs] *Schleimbeutelentzündung* – 17 **sob** [sɒb] *Schluchzen* – 20 **to weep** to cry – 21 **affliction** cause or occasion of suffering – 30 **to embrace** to take (a person) into one's arms – 38 **horsing around** *(sl.)* foolish play, often somewhat wild

**15** 17 **to get a swollen head** to become too proud of o.s. – 22 **frock** dress or gown – 23 **strapped around** attached to – 25 **angelic** [–'– –] like an angel – 27 **perspiring** [pə'spaıərıŋ] sweating – 38 **destitute** ['destıtju:t] extremely poor

**16** 7 **fucking** (vulgar) term often used as a swear word to add emphasis to what is said – 9 **to retrieve** [rı'tri:v] to get back – 11 **to poke out** [pəʊk] to make a hole by pushing s.th. in or through – 14 **Buster!** ['bʌstə] *(sl.)* mister, fellow (has a somewhat rough, insulting connotation) – **whore** (contemptuous term for a) prostitute – 17 **how the hell** *(sl.)* how in the world – **gonna** *(substandard)* going to – 20 **lousy** *(sl.)* disgusting, bad – 23 **orphan** child who has lost one or both of its parents by death – 24 **you bet ...** *(sl.)* sure, certainly – 26 **stinkweed** (weed = *Unkraut*) strong-scented or ill-smelling plant – 28 **self-conscious** [ˌself'kɒnʃəs] insecure, shy – 30 **that figures** *(coll.)* that makes sense – **crumb-bum** a worthless person – **creep** *(sl.)* a disagreeable person – 31 **to bop** *(sl.)* to hit – 33 **I hate your (lousy) guts!** (extremely strong expression of dislike for s.o.) – guts = intestines *(Eingeweide)* – 36 **to apologize** [ə'pɒlədʒaız] to say you are sorry – **ma'am** = madam – 37 **he has no sense of propriety** [prə'praıətı] he doesn't know how to behave – 39 **decency** ['di:snsı] respectable behaviour in society – 40 **to dump** to throw (away) carelessly

**17** 6 **dejectedly** [dı'dʒektıdlı] sadly – 7 **to bow** [baʊ] (done by males) to bend over in a gesture of polite formality – 9 **to curtsy** ['kɛtsı] (done by females) to make a movement of respect (by bending the knees) – **pleased to make your**

**acquaintance** [ə'kweɪntəns] (quite formal) glad to meet you – 11 **to sustain o.s.** [səs'teɪn] to earn money to live – 12 **thespian** ['θespɪən] actor/actress – **tap dancer** *Steptänzer* – **highly regarded chanteuse** highly respected singer – **transitional** [træn'sɪʒənl] changing from one state into another – 15 **genuine ambition** ['dʒenjʊɪn] true desire/goal – **Stock Exchange** *Börse* – 31 **to purchase** to buy – 37 **premature** [ˌpremə'tjʊə] *here:* too early – 38 **foreseeable future** near future

**18** 3 **to be frank with you** quite honestly – 7 **without reservation** without holding back, without doubts – 9 **obligations** responsibilities – 12 **beer-belly** big, fat stomach – 25 **iodine** ['aɪədɪn, *A.E.* 'aɪədaɪn] *Jod* – 28 **to bear** to endure; tolerate – 32 **savior** ['seɪvɪə] (*B.E.* saviour) person who delivers s.o. from harm or danger – 33 **that's a riot** *(sl.)* that's extremely funny

**19** 2 **repressed person** person who suffers from psychological blockages – 8 **shenanigan** *(coll.)* foolery – **willy-nilly** without choice – 9 **brat** (contemptuous) misbehaved child – 10 **gypsy** ['dʒɪpsɪ] *Zigeuner(in)* – 18 **to be the laughing stock** to be laughed at by everyone – 25 **cancer** *Krebs* – 27 **an I.O.U.** (short for:) I owe you = piece of paper in which one acknowledges debt – **lien** [lɪən] a legal claim upon property until the owner has repaid a loan or debt – 31 **to plead** to ask earnestly

**20** 4 **Shirley Temple** famous American child actress in the 1930's – 5 **to pant** to take short, quick breaths – 12 **posture** ['pɒstʃə] way the body is held – 13 **pronounced** strongly marked, distinct – **sophistication** [səˌfɪstɪ'keɪʃn] refined behavior – 15 **to dilly-dally** ['dɪlɪ'dælɪ] to play around – 16 **curt** [kɜ:t] brief, often to the point of rudeness – 19 **clenched** closed tightly – 22 **to da-da** to replace the words of a song with “da” – **to whirl** [wɜ:l] to spin – 23 **to stumble** to fall almost – **noteworthy** ['nəʊtwɜ:ðɪ] significant – 24 **verdict** ['vɜ:dɪkt] judgment, decision – 28 **fervent** ['fɜ:vənt] very passionate

**21** 2 **relentless** [rɪ'lentlɪs] without pity – 16 **bite** *Bissen, Happen* – 20 **incredible** [ɪn'kredɪbl] unbelievable – 22 **head-over-heels** *(coll.)* completely – 17 **casserole** ['kæsərəʊl] food, usually a mixture, cooked in a covered dish of glass or pottery (Auflauf) – 24 **to have one's heart in one's mouth** to be greatly excited or frightened – 25 **over a hundred** (degrees Fahrenheit; about 38.5 centigrade) – 27 **to pinch** *zwicken* – 37 **dedication** [ˌdedɪ'keɪʃn] strong interest in and devotion to s.th.

**22** 1 **incredulous** [ɪn'kredjʊləs] unbelieving – 7 **conservative** *here:* cautiously moderate, not enterprising enough – 12 **simultaneous** [ˌsɪməl'teɪnɪəs, *A.E.* ˌsaɪməl'teɪnɪəs] – 13 **to punctuate** ['pʌŋktjʊeɪt] *here:* to interrupt from time to time

# Interpretation and Teaching Notes

## Content and Analysis

Seated next to his banana-filled pushcart at a New York City waterfront of many years ago is Cornelius J. Hollingsworth the Third, otherwise known as Elias Crapavarnishkes. He arrived yesterday from the old country and is now in business for himself.

Enter Shimmel Shitzman, just off the boat. Shimmel, having heard a rags-to-riches story related to him by Cornelius, is rhapsodical about the great country in which he finds himself. He has, however, one problem: He does not know where to begin. Cornelius decides to help the newly-arrived immigrant, having learned that they were practically neighbors in the old country, and, for a price, offers him American-sounding alternatives to his name. Shimmel does not make a purchase, but does ask Cornelius for advice on finding a job. Cornelius counsels Shimmel to go into business for himself rather than work for somebody else and is ready with advice and encouragement. Shimmel ends up with Cornelius' business, having lost all his money in the transaction.

Shimmel is now on his own in the land of opportunity and very proud of his business. His enthusiasm diminishes, however, when Cornelius reappears with another pushcart, intending to sell at precisely the spot at which Shimmel is located. In spite of the latter's protests, Cornelius refuses to budge, asserting his constitutional rights; he does, however, propose a partnership as a way out of the dilemma. Engaging in offers and counter-offers, a sixty-forty percentage arrangement is worked out (sixty for Cornelius!). After their rather emotional negotiating, they get down to business.

Enter "sweet, angelic" Maggie Cutwell, a poor flower girl pretending to be blind. Feeling sorry for her, Shimmel offers her a banana, only to be met with an outburst somewhat at odds with the flower girl's angelic appearance. Cornelius apologizes for his partner's *faux pas* and proceeds to treat Maggie gallantly. Both say they are engaged in transitional occupations, and their goals lie in the same direction, with Cornelius aspiring to be a theatrical producer, Maggie a dramatic virtuoso.

In the hope that he might be able to use her in one of his productions, Maggie implores Cornelius to give her an audition. She reveals that she is desperate to succeed in her chosen profession and prepared to commit suicide if she does not. Cornelius, pretending to be moved to tears by the story of her life, agrees to let her show him what she can do and sends her off to prepare herself. But he quickly recovers from his emotional involvement in Maggie's story, and is relieved to learn that Shimmel has taken an interest in her, as he, Cornelius, now feels it would be unprofessional to become further involved. Shimmel reluctantly undergoes a name change and emerges as one Sam Stone. Maggie returns to show her stuff. Her talent is not noteworthy. Shimmel, however, has fallen head-over-heels in love with her and declares his determination to make her into a star. The contractual arrangement will be formalized at her apartment in the evening. Shimmel, who hasn't a penny to his name nor a roof over his head, will get a meal out of it and, supposedly, lodging for the night. Maggie goes off to practice – and cook. Cornelius urges Shimmel to be pragmatic, but Shimmel is not daunted. Highly impressed by Shimmel's metamorphosis, Cornelius proposes that they create a corporation. The play ends with Cornelius welcoming Shimmel to America.

Murray Schisgal's *The Pushcart Peddlers* (1980) is a short play which takes as its subject matter the American Dream, making much fun of the notion that an immigrant, any immigrant, "just off the boat" can go from "rags to riches" if only he applies himself. In its humorous treatment of the myth that everyone can – and should – pursue the ideal of the self-made man, the play is unmistakably and assertively American. The play works chiefly with clichés. It is due to Schisgal's comic genius that he could end up with such an entertaining piece.

The myth and reality of the American Dream, however, is not something to be written off as a joke. Although Schisgal takes a humorous approach to the theme, presenting through comedy the absurd aspects of the phenomenon, he offers material which permits a critical reaction.

"Nobody comes to this country to look for a job. There's no future in it. You have to go into business for yourself" (**9** 1–2). Such is the advice our inexperienced immigrant, Shimmel Shitzman, from the vicinity of Kovno-Vilna, Lithuania, receives from the experienced entrepreneur, Cornelius J. Hollingsworth the Third, formerly Elias Crapavarnishkes. "Fantastic! What a country this is!" (**7** 21), Shimmel responds upon hearing Cornelius tell of the man "who arrived here in the morning and owned two factories, three warehouses and a hotel in the Catskill Mountains before he sat down for lunch!" With these lines we have one aspect of the Dream in a nutshell. It is because of their stubborn pursuit of this "rags-to-riches" ideal, the blind faith in the practicability of it all, that Cornelius and Shimmel may be seen in a critical light. For what can be more unadvisable, indeed potentially tragic, than believing in and pursuing a dream – even imagining one has attained it! – wholly at odds with the reality which envelops one?

One's behavior in pursuing the Dream of Success, as is shown in the play, is defined by a concern for appearances, following the assumption that you are what you appear to be. This results in a cultivation of the surface of life and an outright deceptiveness. The first thing Shimmel has to do, he is told, is buy himself an American name, because with a name like Shimmel Shitzman "they'll laugh you out of the country" (**8** 2). When our ignorant immigrant goes by the name of Sam Stone, it is as though he has undergone a remarkable transformation. "I beg to differ with you, Miss Cutwell," says Cornelius. "That *was* Mr. Shitzman. But he has changed considerably since you last saw him" (**20** 10–11).

Maggie, too, is guilty of deliberate deception in her pursuit of stardom. She is neither blind nor "sweet and angelic", as her reprimand "Get your fucking banana off my fucking flowers!" (**16** 7–8), which carries an unmistakable sexual connotation, plainly shows. We notice, however, that she can return instantaneously and at will to her false front when the loss of potential customers is at stake.

A further criticism of the American way, based on Schisgal's treatment of the theme, is that opportunistic behavior is one of the results of subscribing to the Dream of Success. Maggie hardly hesitates to abandon her earlier dislike of Shimmel when she sees that he is prepared to help her reach her goal.

As there is nothing more central to the American experience – past and present – than the notion that the United States is "the land of opportunity", it is appropriate to review a few facts and manifestations of this belief before discussing the play further. This will allow us to better understand the historical reality with which Schisgal is working and against which his comedy is enacted.

As early as 1500, Columbus, after his third voyage, referred to America as a paradise on earth: "the new heaven of the new earth, which Our Lord made [. . .] He made me the messenger and He showed me where to go."[1]

A most famous expression of the hopes of the Puritans, sailing to the New World to escape persecution in England, is that of John Winthrop. In the year 1630, he delivered a sermon entitled *A Model of Christian Charity* in which he declared that the model Christian community "shall be as a city

---

1 Cecil James, ed., *Selected Documents Illustrating the Four Voyages of Columbus,* 1933; quoted in Malk C. Krugmann, "Zur Genese und Struktur des Amerikanismus (I)," *Englisch Amerikanische Studien,* Heft 3 (1979), p. 309.

upon a hill" which should show the world – especially England – how to lead the truly Christian life, adding that "the eyes of all people are upon us."[2] He was referring to the biblical passage: "Ye are the light of the world. A city that is set upon a hill cannot be hid" (Matthew 5:14–15). America is still regarded by many as being a beacon to the rest of the world. Perhaps it will be remembered that Ronald Reagan made use of the phrase "city upon a hill" in talking about America during his campaign for the presidency in 1980.

Another document on the subject is the famous sonnet by the Russian Jewish immigrant Emma Lazarus, engraved on the pedestal of the Statue of Liberty in New York harbor, the gateway to the New World for millions of immigrants. The poem concludes with these lines:

> ... Give me your tired, your poor,
> Your huddled masses yearning to breathe free,
> The wretched refuse of your teeming shore.
> Send these, the homeless, tempest-tost to me,
> I lift my lamp beside the golden door![3]

Horatio Alger's successful and widely read nineteenth-century "rags-to-riches" novels serve to demonstrate the vitality of the Dream of Success at that time. In the preface to his 1874 novel *Risen from the Ranks,* we find an interesting denial of the need for good luck:

> In describing Harry's rise from the ranks I have studiously avoided the extraordinary incidents and pieces of good luck, which the story writer has always at command, being desirous of presenting my hero's career as one which may be imitated by the thousands of boys similarly placed, who, like him, are anxious to rise from the ranks. It is my hope that this story, suggested by the career of an eminent American editor, may afford encouragement to such boys, and teach them that "where there is a will there is a way."[4]

It is interesting to note that the idea of the "self-made man", which is the theme of Alger's novels, is a uniquely American concept in the sense that its connotations are entirely positive. The nearest French equivalents *parvenu* and *nouveau riche,* expressing the European attitude toward this phenomenon, carry a highly negative connotation.

---

2 Ronald Gottesman et. al., eds., *The Norton Anthology of American Literature,* Vol. 1, New York 1979, p. 24.

3 The Reader's Digest Association, Inc., *Family Encyclopedia of American History,* Pleasantville, N.Y., 1975, p. 1065.

4 Quoted in Horst Kruse, ed., *From Rags to Riches: Erfolgsmythos und Erfolgsrezepte in der Amerikanischen Gesellschaft,* München, no date, p. 228.

The reality, of course, was not quite as bright, and any discussion of the American Dream must touch upon this aspect. As for those who came to America hoping to find a land of opportunity, let the following immigrant joke suggest the reality:

> Many immigrants came to America because of the stories they had heard that there the streets were paved with gold. When they got off the boat in New York, however, they discovered three things: first, that the streets were *not* paved with gold, second, that the streets were not paved *at all,* and third, that *they* were expected to pave them.[5]

The Jewish immigrant experience differed greatly from what Schisgal's play seems to suggest at first glance.[6] Of the many Jewish peddlers in New York's East Side, only few managed to set up their own factories and corporations. The vast majority of the immigrant Jews worked hard in the sweatshops of the garment industry and lived in a crowded ghetto. Yet, on a different level, Schisgal's play does portray "reality", as the following quotation may show:

> Go to the great pushcart markets in Hester and Ludlow streets where they join at the northwest corner of Rutgers Square ... and study the people you see there. You will see strange types, but you will also see how strangely Americanized they are becoming, impelled by keen interest and ambition. When you notice that practically everybody is in business, you will understand why practically everybody is, to a greater or less degree, in spirit an American.[7]

And this, indeed, seems to be the play's major theme: "The Americanization of Shimmel Shitzman" might well be its title. *The Pushcart Peddlers* telescopes into one day what took years, in many cases even two generations, to happen in the real world. Much of the play's humor derives from the fact that Shimmel takes to America like a fish to water. His falling in love with Maggie is an indication that he falls in love with and accepts America wholesale, including the crudeness and vulgarity that Maggie stands for.

---

5 Quoted in Brian Tracy and Erwin Helms, eds., *American Dreams – American Nightmares,* Paderborn 1982, p. 33.

6 The following two books are an invaluable source of information on that experience: Irving Howe, *World of our Fathers. The Journey of the East European Jews to America and the Life They Found and Made,* New York 1976 (see particularly the section on peddling, p. 77) and Irving Howe and Kenneth Libo, eds., *How We Lived. A Documentary History of Immigrant Jews in America 1880–1930,* New York 1979.

7 Hutchins Hapgood, *The Spirit of the Ghetto,* New York 1902, quoted in *How We Lived,* p. 65.

The play presents a most remarkable transformation. Shimmel Shitzman, the timid, gullible greenhorn-victim, is transformed within a matter of hours into a most ardent believer in the American way. His "mentor", Cornelius, just can't believe his eyes (**22** 1) and is finally led to admit that Shimmel has outdone him, that he, Cornelius, has been too "conservative" (**22** 7). His final "Welcome to America" (**22** 11) means that there is nothing left that he can teach Shimmel. Shimmel's initiation is complete: an aggressive self-assertiveness (or "keen interest"), ambition and boundless optimism have replaced initial timidity, diffidence and fear of the future.

It is left to the audience/reader to speculate on what "Hollingsworth and Stone, Inc." will concentrate its future business activities on: Will it specialize in "initiating" further newly arrived greenhorns or will it strike out to tackle more meaningful tasks? But, then, who is to judge if the initiation of greenhorns, however painful to them, is not in itself a meaningful pursuit?

There is an interesting common denominator in Miller's *Death of a Salesman* and Schisgal's *Pushcart Peddlers,* in that both set up a tension between what is desired and asserted, and what is actually achieved. However, Schisgal, unlike Miller, is not the least bit interested in exploring the tragic potential inherent in this conflict. Also it can be argued that Schisgal's play is set in a period "many years ago" (**5** 8), when the Dream of Success still held out its promise. Willy Loman, on the other hand, is a latter-day pursuer of the Dream turned sour.

*The Pushcart Peddlers* is an extraordinarily funny play. As it clearly makes fun of the theme of the American Dream, it is tempting to see it as a satire on the phenomenon. However, the play is not so much a satire with the purpose of exposing a foible or vice in order to criticize or correct as it is a good-natured burlesque.

Shimmel's emergence from apprenticeship at the end, surpassing even Cornelius in boldly seizing opportunity and asserting that success is within one's grasp, is a delightful development. He is set up at the beginning as the model of naïveté and shyness, while Cornelius seems to know all the tricks; his metamorphosis comes as a nice surprise.

Although appearing to offer a satire on the American Dream, especially the blind pursuit of the Dream of Success, Schisgal is actually more interested in entertaining than anything else. *The Pushcart Peddlers* is a delightful romantic comedy, not only because it involves a "love story" at the end, but also because it creates a make-believe world where the fantastic is at least asserted. The discrepancy between dream and reality is not the least bit important. That Shimmel, just off the boat, speaks English fluently, that Cornelius speaks of the rush hour when he is virtually alone and that Maggie most certainly will not attain stardom is all entirely irrelevant.

## First Unit: Make-Believe and Reality

As there are no serious language problems to be expected, even less advanced students should be able to prepare the first scene – the first ten pages, that is – at home. Ideally, if students are used to listening comprehension, we suggest listening to the first scene (until Maggie enters) on cassette to take advantage of the highly entertaining recording and thus arouse curiosity.

1. *What is funny about the play? What made you smile?*
The students will answer something along the line of, "the protagonists pretend to be businessmen, but they are not; they have just arrived but seem to know everything about big business." A clash between make-believe and reality, desire and truth will be detected. If the protagonists' appearance, financial situation, and social status is examined in a closer reading of the first four pages, one will easily get an impression of what the reality of their situation is like (cf. board).

2. *What do the protagonists desire? How do they judge their situation?*
The clash between reality and make-believe can be portrayed on the board:

| | reality/truth | pretense/desire |
|---|---|---|
| appearance | threadbare clothes<br>battered suitcase | proprietary air (**11** 10) |
| location | N. Y. City waterfront<br>trash cans | "great country"<br>beautiful day |
| business | penniless<br>jobless<br>no customers (except for Shimmel) | excellent business<br>rush hour |
| social status | immigrants | pretentious American names |

**Homework**
Write a summary of the first part of the play. Use the following expressions:

(the play) opens; (it is) set; protagonists; subject matter; to be in business; to engage in offers; to negotiate.

In order to make it evident that this "fictional" clash between desire and reality corresponds to the actual historical situation, it becomes necessary to review certain facts. Whether the teacher guides the students by presenting the historical facts in chronological order, or whether the events mentioned by the students are just illustrated or organized, depends upon the knowledge of the class. The teacher will of course have the freedom to focus on other details than the ones listed here, depending on the respective curriculum or field of interest. In any case, the following scheme and blackboard sketch may be considered:

3. *Arnold Schwarzenegger has said of America: "It is the country where you can turn your dream into reality. Other countries don't have those things. When I came over here to America, I felt I was in heaven. In America, we don't have an obstacle. Nobody's holding you back."*[8] *How did America develop this kind of reputation?*
List events according to blackboard scheme, American Dream.

4. *Reality, of course, has its darker sides. Give examples.*

| **Historical reality** | **American Dream** |
|---|---|
| • existence of slavery (until 1865)<br>• immigrants exploited as cheap laborers; poverty<br>• slum dwellings of the lower East Side<br>• discrimination against minorities | • Columbus' vision of a paradise on earth in the New World (1500).<br>• Puritans' hope for religious freedom and independence (17th century)<br>• immigrants' dream of freedom and economic success<br>• dreams of a land where you can rise on your own merit, be a self-made man<br>• land of unlimited opportunity |

clash between America's historical reality and the American Dream

**Homework**
Prepare the rest of the play and underline passages that serve to illustrate Maggie's character and behavior best.

8 Studs Terkel, *American Dreams: Lost and Found,* New York 1980, p. 127.

5. *Describe the difference between Maggie's "public" behavior and her "private" behavior. Compare the following lines:* **15** *25–38;* **16** *7–34.*

**Maggie and her dream of success**

| **public behavior** | **Maggie in private** |
|---|---|
| • sweet, angelic voice (suggesting innocence) | • curses, uses foul language with sexual connotations |
| • flower girl | |
| • beautiful looks | |
| • blind | • can see |
| • looks destitute | • is not hungry |
| • evokes sympathy | • can take care of herself; abuses people who show sympathy if she does not financially or professionally profit from them |

↓ pretentious behavior in order to succeed

6. *Describe her feelings towards Shimmel.*
She dislikes him as long as she feels she cannot profit from him, but doesn't hesitate to abandon her dislike when she realizes that he may be useful. The former "crumb-bum" and "creep" becomes her potential lover. Feelings are secondary to professional success.

**Homework**
Write a summary of the second part of the play. (This homework could also be assigned after the next unit.)

## Second Unit: The Writer's Intention and the Characters in the Play

1. *What are the characters' ultimate goals?*
They want "big business", property and stardom.

2. *How do the protagonists intend to get there?*
Opportunistic and pretentious behavior seems to be most promising.

3. *Can we conclude from this what the writer's intentions were?*
By portraying their goals as being obviously contradictory to the reality in which they are situated, Schisgal shows his characters in a very critical light (e.g. the continuous assertion that business is great even though it has not exactly been inundated with customers, or Maggie's ambitions which lie in

a field where she has no talent). Furthermore, Schisgal ridicules and criticizes not only their goals but the protagonists themselves who naïvely believe in the Dream and stubbornly pursue it (e.g. the rags-to-riches story and Shimmel's naïve response to it).

First and foremost, however, Schisgal quite obviously intends to entertain the audience through exaggerations (e.g. Cornelius' American name, the extreme transformations Maggie undergoes) and by deliberately treating a potentially very serious topic so lightly.

4. *List more comic effects of the play.*
- the rather comic character development from naïveté to "knowing the game" in Shimmel's case
- the romantic ending
- "tough" Cornelius falling for Maggie's sob story against his will
- a banana pushcart representing the idea, the dream, of big business

The terms "satire" and "comedy" could be introduced and discussed in this context:

> SATIRE is the literary art of diminishing a subject by making it ridiculous and evoking toward it attitudes of amusement, contempt, indignation, or scorn. It differs from the comic in that comedy evokes laughter as an end in itself, while satire "derides"; that is, it uses laughter as a weapon, and against a butt existing outside the work itself. That butt may be an individual (in "personal satire"), or a type of person, a class, an institution, a nation, or even ... the whole race of man. The distinction between the comic and the satiric, however, is a sharp one only at its extremes.
>
> COMEDY. A comedy is a work in which the materials are selected and managed primarily in order to interest and amuse us: the characters and their discomfitures engage our delighted attention rather than our profound concern, we feel confident that no great disaster will occur, and usually the action turns out happily for the chief characters. The term "comedy" is customarily applied only to dramas; it should be noted, however, that the comic form, so defined, also occurs in prose fiction and narrative poetry.[9]

5. *Describe the characters in the drama. How do they develop? What individualizing details are presented? Are they complex, difficult to understand, or not?*

The characters are rather simple, serving only the idea of illustrating the naïve pursuit of a naïve dream. (Shimmel's rather quick metamorphosis

---

9 M. H. Abrams, *A Glossary of Literary Terms,* New York 1971, pp. 153, 25.

from ignorance and innocence to an understanding of business is hardly rooted in the complexity of his character.)

E. M. Forster's terms discriminating between "flat" and "round" characters, introduced in *Aspects of the Novel* (1927), may be explained to the students in this context:

> A flat character (also called a "type," or "two-dimensional") is built around "a single idea or quality" and is presented in outline and without much individualizing detail, and so can be fairly accurately described in a single phrase or sentence. A round character is complex in temperament and motivation and is represented with subtle particularity; thus he is difficult to describe with any accuracy as a person in real life, and, like most people, he is capable of surprising us. Almost all dramas and narratives, properly enough, have some characters who serve as mere functionaries and are not characterized at all, as well as other characters who are quite flat: there is no need, in Shakespeare's *Henry IV, Part 1,* for Mistress Quickly to be as globular as Falstaff. The degree to which a character needs to be three-dimensional depends on his function in the plot, and in many types of plot, such as in a detective novel or adventure novel or farce comedy, even the protagonist usually possesses only two dimensions. Sherlock Holmes and Long John Silver do not require, for their own excellent literary roles, the roundedness of a Hamlet, a Becky Sharp, or a Jay Gatsby ...[10]

## Third Unit: The Americanization of Shimmel Shitzman

1. *As we have found out, the Dream of Success and Schisgal's mild criticism of this idea is one of the themes of the play. What other theme can we detect? Consider the transformation of Shimmel Shitzman.*
We witness the transformation of Shimmel Shitzman from naïve, timid immigrant to self-assertive, optimistic businessman. We might say that the play retraces the Americanization of one immigrant.

2. *Retrace step by step Shimmel's Americanization.*
- Initiation into the proper way of selling things from a pushcart (**9** 29–**10** 8).
- The fact of all-out competition in America (**11** 33–**12** 5).
- How to "negotiate" (**13** 3–12).
- How to deal with "ladies" (**17** 31–35).
- Acquiring an American name (**19** 39) and learning to live up to it ("That's it. Feel Stone. Feel rock. Feel hard. Feel firm. Feel strong." **20** 2–3).

---

10 *Ibid,* p. 21.

- Shimmel acquires pronounced certainty and sophistication (**20** 12–13).
- Shimmel has learned that "time is money" ("We don't have all day to dilly-dally" **20** 15).

3. *What role does Cornelius play in this process?*
Shimmel is the novice, the innocent greenhorn who has to be taught the ways of the New World. Cornelius assumes this role of mentor or teacher, though not for unselfish reasons. Cornelius, it seems, makes a living of cheating newly arrived immigrants out of the little money they have. In return the "pupils" acquire knowledge about how to survive in a competitive American environment so different from the old country they have just left.

4. *What is Maggie's role in this respect?*
She functions as a kind of barometer which measures Shimmel's progress. Her complete rejection of Shimmel in the beginning changes into gratitude and a measure of admiration when she realizes that Shimmel has acquired not only an acceptable name but also some of those qualities which are a prerequisite for success in the American environment.

5. *Consider the names of the characters and the names Cornelius offers to "sell" to Shimmel* (**8** 21–23). *Do they carry any connotations?*
Crapavarnishkes, "not a bad name" (**8** 5) to Shimmel before his Americanization, and Shitzman are indeed names that will at least bring a smile on an English-speaking person's face (consider the first syllable of both).

Cornelius J. Hollingsworth III is an ingenious replacement for the former name. Cornelius, being the given name of Cornelius Vanderbilt (1794–1877; railroad magnate and one of the richest men in America at that time), suggests riches and business connections. Without a middle initial, any "good" American name would be incomplete. Hollingsworth sounds very English and suggests that the forefathers of the name's bearer might have been among the first to settle the country. The addition of "the Third", finally, is indicative of a family that is tradition-minded. (In some American families the eldest son is given his father's name.)

Maggie Cutwell has an unpretentious American name. Her surname is possibly suggestive of her sharp, "cutting" manner.

Andrew Hamilton (**8** 21): there was an American lawyer by that name, but what Schisgal is probably playing on here is the combination of Andrew Carnegie's (see below) given name and Alexander Hamilton's surname. Hamilton (1755–1804) played a very prominent part during the American Revolution and the early years of the nation.

Sylvester Peterson (**8** 21): a name that sounds very dignified and English.

Thomas Hathaway (**8** 22): a thoroughly English name (Hathaway was Shakespeare's wife's maiden name).

Roger Williams Carnegie (**8** 22): a composite of two very American names. Roger Williams was the founder of the Colony of Rhode Island (1644); he was a staunch proponent of religious liberty and was known for his friendly treatment of the Indians. Andrew Carnegie (1835–1919), born in Scotland, emigrated to the United States as a penniless boy and became one of the richest men in America and the world.

Samuel P. Stone (**8** 23): Samuel Stone was an English nonconformist who emigrated to America in 1633, where he later founded the town of Hartford in Connecticut. Apart from this, Stone is a rather ordinary American name. Samuel was the given name of three signers of the Declaration of Independence (Samuel Adams being the best known of the three).

6. *Comment on the last words spoken in the play: "Welcome to America".*
With these words Cornelius acknowledges that there is no more that he can teach Shimmel, that he accepts him as an equal. They are in a way similar to a high school diploma sealing Shimmel's initiation.

7. *Consider the duration of the action. What has Murray Schisgal tried to do?*
The play telescopes a development which normally took years if not two or more generations into a few hours: the transformation of tradition-oriented East European immigrants into "hardnosed" businessmen who are capable of holding their own in a society whose values are so different from those of their forefathers. Much of the play's humor stems from this accelerated pace.

8. *For discussion: How do you think a Jewish American audience would react to the play?*

**Homework**

Write an essay on *The Pushcart Peddlers.* (What is the theme and subject matter? How is it approached? What is the author's intention? How do you personally appreciate the play?)

## For Further Study and Discussion

1. There are several collections of texts dealing with the American Dream and with immigration on the market, e. g. *American Dreams – American Nightmares* (Schöningh) and *The American Dream – Past and Present* (Klettbuch 51361).

2. Listen to the cassette and follow Cornelius' use of legal terminology and business concepts throughout the play. List the terms and discuss the underlying concept.

3. List terms having to do with immigration.
The following list should be completed by the teacher and the class:
to emigrate/emigration (leave a country)
to immigrate/immigration (enter a country)
to admit/accept; limit/raise the number of immigrants from ...
to pass immigration laws
entrant
to tighten entry requirements/rules
foreign/guest workers
to deport (illegal) aliens
to become a (permanent) resident
to grant citizenship
refugees (come into a country)
to apply for/grant political asylum

4. Discuss the situation of today's migrants in the U.S.A. and West Germany. What do you know about current legal proceedings, problems, attitudes, expectations regarding the migrants?

Thornton Wilder

# The Happy Journey to Trenton and Camden

Characters

THE STAGE MANAGER
MA KIRBY
ARTHUR *(thirteen)*
CAROLINE *(fifteen)*
PA (ELMER) KIRBY
BEULAH *(twenty-two)*

*No scenery is required for this play. The idea is that no place is being represented. This may be achieved by a gray curtain back-drop with no side-pieces; a cyclorama; or the empty bare stage.*

*(As the curtain rises the stage manager is leaning lazily against the proscenium pillar at the left. He is smoking. Arthur is playing marbles down center in pantomime. Caroline is way up left talking to some girls who are invisible to us. Ma Kirby is anxiously putting on her hat [real] before an imaginary mirror up right.)*

MA Where's your pa? Why isn't he here? I declare we'll never get started.
ARTHUR Ma, where's my hat? I guess I don't go if I can't find my hat.

*(Still playing marbles.)*

MA Go out into the hall and see if it isn't there. Where's Caroline gone to now, the plagued child?
ARTHUR She's out waitin' in the street talkin' to the Jones girls. – I just looked in the hall a thousand times, Ma, and it isn't there. *(He spits for good luck before a difficult shot and mutters.)* Come on, baby.
MA Go and look again, I say. Look carefully.

*(Arthur rises, relucantly, crosses right, turns around, returns swiftly to his game center, flinging himself on the floor with a terrible impact, and starts shooting an aggie.)*

ARTHUR No, Ma, it's not there.

MA *(serenely):* Well, you don't leave Newark without that hat, make up your mind to that. I don't go on journeys with a hoodlum.

ARTHUR Aw, Ma!

*(Ma comes down right to the footlights, pulls up an imaginary window and talks toward the audience.)*

MA *(calling):* Oh, Mrs. Schwartz!

THE STAGE MANAGER *(down left. Consulting his script):* Here I am, Mrs. Kirby. Are you going yet?

MA I guess we're going in just a minute. How's the baby?

THE STAGE MANAGER She's all right now. We slapped her on the back and she spat it up.

MA Isn't that fine! – Well, now, if you'll be good enough to give the cat a saucer of milk in the morning and the evening, Mrs. Schwartz, I'll be ever so grateful to you. – Oh, good-afternoon, Mrs. Hobmeyer!

THE STAGE MANAGER Good-afternoon, Mrs. Kirby, I hear you're going away.

MA *(modest):* Oh, just for three days, Mrs. Hobmeyer, to see my married daughter, Beulah, in Camden. Elmer's got his vacation week from the laundry early this year, and he's just the best driver in the world.

*(Caroline comes down stage right and stands by her mother.)*

THE STAGE MANAGER Is the whole family going?

MA Yes, all four of us that's here. The change ought to be good for the children. My married daughter was downright sick a while ago –

THE STAGE MANAGER Tchk – tchk – tchk! Yes. I remember you tellin' us.

MA *(with feeling):* And I just want to go down and see the child. I ain't seen her since then. I just won't rest easy in my mind without I see her. (To Caroline) Can't you say good-afternoon to Mrs. Hobmeyer?

CAROLINE *(lowers her eyes and says woodenly):* Good-afternoon, Mrs. Hobmeyer.

THE STAGE MANAGER Good-afternoon, dear. – Well, I'll wait and beat these rugs until after you're gone, because I don't want to choke you. I hope you have a good time and find everything all right.

MA Thank you, Mrs. Hobmeyer, I hope I will. – Well, I guess that milk for the cat is all, Mrs. Schwartz, if you're sure you don't mind. If anything should come up, the key to the back door is hanging by the ice-box.

CAROLINE Ma! Not so loud.

ARTHUR Everybody can hear yuh.

MA Stop pullin' my dress, children. *(In a loud whisper.)* The key to the back door I'll leave hangin' by the ice-box and I'll leave the screen unhooked.

THE STAGE MANAGER Now have a good trip, dear, and give my love to Beuhly.

MA I will, and thank you a thousand times. *(She lowers the window, turns up stage, and looks around. Caroline goes left and vigorously rubs her cheeks. Ma occupies herself with the last touches of packing.)* What can be keeping your pa?

ARTHUR *(who has not left his marbles):* I can't find my hat, Ma.

*(Enter Elmer holding a cap, up right.)*

ELMER Here's Arthur's hat. He musta left it in the car Sunday.

MA That's a mercy. Now we can start. – Caroline Kirby, what you done to your cheeks?

CAROLINE *(defiant-abashed):* Nothin'.

MA If you've put anything on 'em, I'll slap you.

CAROLINE No, Ma, of course I haven't. *(Hanging her head.)* I just rubbed 'm to make 'm red. All the girls do that at High School when they're goin' places.

MA Such silliness I never saw. Elmer, what kep' you?

ELMER *(always even-voiced and always looking out a little anxiously through his spectacles):* I just went to the garage and had Charlie give a last look at it, Kate.

MA I'm glad you did. *Collecting two pieces of imaginary luggage and starting for the door.)* I wouldn't like to have no breakdown miles from anywhere. Now we can start. Arthur, put those marbles away. Anybody'd think you didn't want to go on a journey to look at yuh.

*(They go out through the "hall". Ma opens imaginary door down right. Pa, Caroline, and Arthur go through it. Ma follows, taking time to lock the door, hang the key by the "ice-box." They turn up at an abrupt angle, going up stage. As they come to the steps from the back porch, each arriving at a given point, starts bending his knees lower and lower to denote going downstairs, and find themselves in the street. The stage manager moves from the right to the automobile. It is right center of the stage, seen partially at an angle, its front pointing down center.*

ELMER *(coming forward):* Here, you boys, you keep away from that car.

MA Those Sullivan boys put their heads into everything.

*(They get into the car. Elmer's hands hold an imaginary steering wheel and continually shift gears. Ma sits beside him. Arthur is behind him and Caroline is behind Ma.)*

CAROLINE *(standing up in the back seat, waving self-consciously):* Good-bye, Mildred. Good-bye, Helen.

THE STAGE MANAGER *(having returned to his position by the left proscenium):* Good-bye, Caroline. Good-bye, Mrs. Kirby. I hope y' have a good time.

MA Good-bye, girls.

THE STAGE MANAGER Good-bye, Kate. The car looks fine.

MA *(looking upward toward a window right):* Oh, good-bye, Emma! *(Modestly.)* We think it's the best little Chevrolet in the world. – *(Looking up toward the left.)* Oh, good-bye, Mrs. Adler!

THE STAGE MANAGER What, are you going away, Mrs. Kirby?

MA Just for three days, Mrs. Adler, to see my married daughter in Camden.

THE STAGE MANAGER Have a good time.

*(Now Ma, Caroline, and the Stage Manager break out into a tremendous chorus of good-byes. The whole street is saying good-bye. Arthur takes out his pea shooter and lets fly happily into the air. There is a lurch or two and they are off.)*

ARTHUR *(leaning forward in sudden fright):* Pa! Pa! Don't go by the school. Mr. Biedenbach might see us!

MA I don't care if he does see us. I guess I can take my children out of school for one day without having to hide down back streets about it. *(Elmer nods to a passerby. Without sharpness.)* Who was that you spoke to, Elmer?

ELMER That was the fellow who arranges our banquets down to the Lodge, Kate.

MA Is he the one who had to buy four hundred steaks? *(Pa nods.)* I declare, I'm glad I'm not him.

ELMER The air's getting better already. Take deep breaths, children.

*(They inhale noisily.)*

ARTHUR *(pointing to a sign and indicating that it gradually goes by):* Gee, it's almost open fields already. *"Weber and Heilbroner Suits for Well-dressed Men."* Ma, can I have one of them some day?

MA If you graduate with good marks perhaps your father'll let you have one for graduation.

*(Pause. General gazing about, then sudden lurch.)*

CAROLINE *(whining):* Oh, Pa! do we have to wait while that whole funeral goes by?

*(Elmer takes off his hat. Ma cranes forward with absorbed curiosity.)*

MA *(not sharp and bossy):* Take off your hat, Arthur. Look at your father. – Why, Elmer, I do believe that's a lodge-brother of yours. See the banner? I suppose this is the Elizabeth branch. *(Elmer nods. Ma sighs: Tchk-tchk-tchk. The children lean forward and all watch the funeral in silence, growing momentarily more solemnized. After a pause, Ma continues almost dreamily but not sentimentally.)* Well, we haven't forgotten the funeral that we went on, have we? We haven't forgotten our good Harold. He gave his life for this country, we mustn't forget that. *(There is another pause; with cheerful resignation.)* Well, we'll all hold up the traffic for a few minutes some day.

THE CHILDREN *(very uncomfortable):* Ma!

MA *(without self-pity):* Well, I'm "ready," children. I hope everybody in this car is "ready." And I pray to go first, Elmer. Yes.

*(Elmer touches her hand.)*

CAROLINE Ma, everybody's looking at you.

ARTHUR Everybody's laughing at you.

MA Oh, hold your tongues! I don't care what a lot of silly people in Elizabeth, New Jersey, think of me. – Now we can go on. That's the last.

*(There is another lurch and the car goes on.)*

CAROLINE *(looking at a sign and turning as she passes it): "Fit-Rite Suspenders. The Working Man's Choice."* Pa, why do they spell Rite that way?

ELMER So that it'll make you stop and ask about it, Missy.

CAROLINE Papa, you're teasing me. – Ma, why do they say *"Three Hundred Rooms Three Hundred Baths"?*

ARTHUR *"Miller's Spaghetti: The Family's Favorite Dish."* Ma, why don't you ever have spaghetti?

MA Go along, you'd never eat it.

ARTHUR Ma, I like it now.

CAROLINE *(with gesture):* Yum-yum. It looked wonderful up there. Ma, make some when we get home?

MA *(dryly):* "The management is always happy to receive suggestions. We aim to please."

*(The children scream with laughter. Even Elmer smiles. Ma remains modest.)*

ELMER Well, I guess no one's complaining, Kate. Everybody knows you're a good cook.

MA I don't know whether I'm a good cook or not, but I know I've had practice. At least I've cooked three meals a day for twenty-five years.

ARTHUR Aw, Ma, you went out to eat once in a while.

MA Yes. That made it a leap year.

*(The children laugh again.)*

CAROLINE *(in an ecstasy of well-being puts her arms around her mother):* Ma, I love going out in the country like this. Let's do it often, Ma.

MA Goodness, smell that air, will you! It's got the whole ocean in it. – Elmer, drive careful over that bridge. This must be New Brunswick we're coming to.

ARTHUR *(after a slight pause):* Ma, when is the next comfort station?

MA *(unruffled):* You don't want one. You just said that to be awful.

CAROLINE *(shrilly):* Yes, he did, Ma. He's terrible. He says that kind of thing right out in school and I want to sink through the floor, Ma. He's terrible.

MA Oh, don't get so excited about nothing, Miss Proper! I guess we're all yewman beings in this car, at least as far as I know. And, Arthur, you try and be a gentleman. – Elmer, don't run over that collie dog. *She follows the dog with her eyes.)* Looked kinda peaked to me. Needs a good honest bowl of leavings. Pretty dog, too. *(Her eyes fall on a billboard at the right.)* That's a pretty advertisement for Chesterfield cigarettes, isn't it? Looks like Beulah, a little.

ARTHUR Ma?

MA Yes.

ARTHUR *("route" rhymes with "out"):* Can't I take a paper route with the Newark *Daily Post?*

MA No, you cannot. No, sir. I hear they make the paper boys get up four-thirty in the morning. No son of mine is going to get up at four-thirty every morning, not if it's to make a million dollars. Your *Saturday Evening Post* route on Thursday mornings is enough.

ARTHUR Aw, Ma.

MA No, sir. No son of mine is going to get up at four-thirty and miss the sleep God meant him to have.

ARTHUR *(sullenly):* Hhm! Ma's always talking about God. I guess she got a letter from Him this morning.

MA *(outraged):* Elmer, stop that automobile this minute. I don't go another step with anybody that says things like that. Arthur, you get out of this car. *(Elmer stops the car.)* Elmer, you give him a dollar bill. He can go back to Newark by himself. I don't want him.

ARTHUR What did I say? There wasn't anything terrible about that.

ELMER I didn't hear what he said, Kate.

MA God has done a lot of things for me and I won't have Him made fun of by anybody. Get out of this car this minute.

CAROLINE Aw, Ma – don't spoil the ride.

MA No.

ELMER We might as well go on, Kate, since we've got started. I'll talk to the boy tonight.

MA *(slowly conceding):* All right, if you say so, Elmer.

*(Elmer starts the car.)*

ARTHUR *(frightened):* Aw, Ma, that wasn't so terrible.

MA I don't want to talk about it. I hope your father washes your mouth out with soap and water. – Where'd we all be if I started talking about God like that, I'd like to know! We'd be in the speakeasies and nightclubs and places like that, that's where we'd be.

CAROLINE *(after a very slight pause):* What did he say, Ma? I didn't hear what he said.

MA I don't want to talk about it.

*(They drive on in silence for a moment, the shocked silence after a scandal.)*

ELMER I'm going to stop and give the car a little water, I guess.

MA All right, Elmer. You know best.

ELMER *(turns the wheel and stops; as to a garage hand)* Could I have a little water in the radiator – to make sure?

THE STAGE MANAGER *(in this scene alone he lays aside his script and enters into a rôle seriously)* You sure can. *(He punches the left front tire.)* Air all right? Do you need any oil or gas?

*(Goes up around car.)*

ELMER No, I think not. I just got fixed up in Newark.

*(The Stage Manager carefully pours some water into the hood.)*

MA We're on the right road for Camden, are we?

THE STAGE MANAGER *(coming down on right side of car)* Yes, keep straight ahead. You can't miss it. You'll be in Trenton in a few minutes. Camden's a great town, lady, believe me.

MA My daughter likes it fine – my married daughter.

THE STAGE MANAGER Ye'? It's a great burg all right. I guess I think so because I was born near there.

MA Well, well. Your folks still live there?

THE STAGE MANAGER *(standing with one foot on the rung of Ma's chair. They have taken a great fancy to one another)* No, my old man sold the farm and they built a factory on it. So the folks moved to Philadelphia.

MA My married daughter Beulah lives there because her husband works in the telephone company. – Stop pokin' me, Caroline! – We're all going down to see her for a few days.

THE STAGE MANAGER Ye'?

MA She's been sick, you see, and I just felt I had to go and see her. My husband and my boy are going to stay at the Y.M.C.A. I hear they've got a dormitory on the top floor that's real clean and comfortable. Have you ever been there?

THE STAGE MANAGER No. I'm Knights of Columbus myself.

MA Oh.

THE STAGE MANAGER I used to play basketball at the Y though. It looked all right to me. *(He reluctantly moves away and pretends to examine the car again.)* Well, I guess you're all set now, lady. I hope you have a good trip; you can't miss it.

EVERYBODY Thanks. Thanks a lot. Good luck to you.

*(Jolts and lurches.)*

MA *(with a sigh)* The world's full of nice people. – That's what I call a nice young man.

CAROLINE *(earnestly)* Ma, you oughtn't to tell 'm all everything about yourself.

MA Well, Caroline, you do your way and I'll do mine. – He looked kinda pale to me. I'd like to feed him up for a few days. His mother lives in Philadelphia and I expect he eats at those dreadful Greek places.

CAROLINE I'm hungry. Pa, there's a hot dog stand. K'n I have one?

ELMER We'll all have one, eh, Kate? We had such an early lunch.

MA Just as you think best, Elmer.

*(Elmer stops the car.)*

ELMER Arthur, here's half a dollar. – Run over and see what they have. Not too much mustard either.

*(Arthur descends from the car and goes off stage right. Ma and Caroline get out and walk a bit, up stage and to the left. Caroline keeps at her mother's right.)*

MA What's that flower over there? – I'll take some of those to Beulah.

CAROLINE It's just a weed, Ma.

MA I like it. – My, look at the sky, wouldya! I'm glad I was born in New Jersey. I've always said it was the best state in the Union. Every state has something no other state has got.

*(Presently Arthur returns with his hands full of imaginary hot dogs which he distributes. First to his father, next to Caroline, who comes forward to meet him, and lastly to his mother. He is still very much cast down by the recent scandal, and as he approaches his mother says falteringly):*

ARTHUR Ma, I'm sorry. I'm sorry. I'm sorry for what I said.

*(He bursts into tears.)*

MA There. There. We all say wicked things at times. I know you didn't mean it like it sounded. *(He weeps still more violently than before.)* Why, now, now! I forgive you, Arthur, and tonight before you go to bed you ... *(She whispers.)* You're a good boy at heart, Arthur, and we all know it. *(Caroline starts to cry too. Ma is suddenly joyously alive and happy.)* Sakes alive, it's too nice a day for us all to be cryin'. Come now, get in. *(Crossing behind car to the right side, followed by the children.)* Caroline, go up in front with your father. Ma wants to sit with her beau. *(Caroline sits in front with her father. Ma lets Arthur get in car ahead of her; then she closes door.)* I never saw such children. Your hot dogs are all getting wet. Now chew them fine, everybody. – All right, Elmer, forward march. *(Car starts. Caroline spits.)* Caroline, whatever are you doing?

CAROLINE I'm spitting out the leather, Ma.

MA Then say: Excuse me.

CAROLINE Excuse me, please.

*(She spits again.)*

MA What's this place? Arthur, did you see the post office?

ARTHUR It said Lawrenceville.

MA Hhn. School kinda. Nice. I wonder what that big yellow house set back was. – Now it's beginning to be Trenton.

CAROLINE Papa, it was near here that George Washington crossed the Delaware. It was near Trenton, Mama. He was first in war and first in peace, and first in the hearts of his countrymen.

MA *(surveying the passing world, serene and didactic)* Well the thing I like about him best was that he never told a lie. *(The children are duly cast down. There is a pause. Arthur stands up and looks at the car ahead.)* There's a sunset for you. There's nothing like a good sunset.

ARTHUR There's an Ohio license in front of us. Ma, have you ever been to Ohio?

MA No.

*(A dreamy silence descends upon them. Caroline sits closer to her father, toward the left; Arthur closer to Ma on the right, who puts her arm around him, unsentimentally.)*

ARTHUR Ma, what a lotta people there are in the world, Ma. There must be thousands and thousands in the United States. Ma, how many are there?

MA I don't know. Ask your father.

ARTHUR Pa, how many are there?

ELMER There are a hundred and twenty-six million, Kate.

MA *(giving a pressure about Arthur's shoulder)* And they all like to drive out in the evening with their children beside 'm. Why doesn't somebody sing something? Arthur, you're always singing something; what's the matter with you?

ARTHUR All right. What'll we sing?

*(He sketches.)*

In the Blue Ridge Mountains of Virginia,
On the …

No, I don't like that anymore. Let's do:

I been workin' on de railroad
*(Caroline joins in.)*
All de liblong day.
*(Ma sings.)*
I been workin' on de railroad
*(Elmer joins in.)*

Just to pass de time away.
Don't you hear de whistle blowin', etc.

*(Ma suddenly jumps up with a wild cry and a large circular gesture.)*

MA Elmer, that signpost said Camden. I saw it.

ELMER All right, Kate, if you're sure.

*(Much shifting of gears, backing, and jolting.)*

MA Yes, there it is. Camden – five miles. Dear old Beulah. *(The journey continues.)* Now, children, you be good and quiet during dinner. She's just got out of bed after a big sorta operation, and we must all move around kinda quiet. First you drop me and Caroline at the door and just say hello, and the you men-folk go over to the Y.M.C.A. and come back for dinner in about an hour.

CAROLINE *(shutting her eyes and pressing her fists passionately against her nose)* I see the first star. Everybody make a wish.

Star light, star bright,
First star I seen tonight.
I wish I may, I wish I might
Have the wish I wish tonight.

*(Then solemnly.)* Pins. Mama, you say "needles."

*(She interlocks little fingers with her mother across back of seat.)*

MA Needles.

CAROLINE Shakespeare. Ma, you say "Longfellow."

MA Longfellow.

CAROLINE Now it's a secret and I can't tell it to anybody. Ma, you make a wish.

MA *(with almost grim humor)* No, I can make wishes without waiting for no star. And I can tell my wishes right out loud too. Do you want to hear them?

CAROLINE *(resignedly)* No, Ma, we know 'm already. We've heard 'm. *(She hangs her head affectedly on her left shoulder and says with unmalicious mimicry.)* You want me to be a good girl and you want Arthur to be honest-in-word-and-deed.

MA *(majestically)* Yes. So mind yourself.

ELMER Caroline, take out that letter from Beulah in my coat pocket by you and read aloud the places I marked with red pencil.

CAROLINE *(laboriously making it out)* *"A few blocks after you pass the two big oil tanks on your left ..."*

EVERYBODY *(pointing backward)* There they are!

CAROLINE *"... you come to a corner where there's an A and P store on the left and a firehouse kitty-corner to it ..." (They all jubilantly identify these landmarks.) "... turn right, go two blocks and our house is Weyerhauser St. Number 471."*

MA It's an even nicer street than they used to live in. And right handy to an A and P.

CAROLINE *(whispering)* Ma, it's better than our street. It's richer than our street. Ma, isn't Beulah richer than we are?

MA *(looking at her with a firm and glassy eye)* Mind yourself, Missy. I don't want to hear anybody talking about rich or not rich when I'm around. If people aren't nice I don't care how rich they are. I live in the best street in the world because my husband and children live there. *(She glares impressively at Caroline a moment to let this lesson sink in, then looks up, sees Beulah off left, and waves.)* There's Beulah standing on the steps looking for us.

*(Beulah enters from left, also waving. They all call out: "Hello, Beulah – hello." Presently they are all getting out of the car, except Elmer, busy with brakes.)*

BEULAH Hello, Mamma. Well, lookit how Arthur and Caroline are growing.

MA They're bursting all their clothes.

BEULAH *(crossing in front of them and kissing her father long and affectionately)* Hello, Papa. Good old papa. You look tired, Pa.

MA Yes, your pa needs a rest. Thank Heaven, his vacation has come just now. We'll feed him up and let him sleep late. *(Elmer gets out of car and stands in front of it.)* Pa has a present for you, Loolie. He would go and buy it.

BEULAH Why, Pa, you're terrible to go and buy anything for me. Isn't he terrible?

*(Stage Manager removes automobile.)*

MA Well, it's a secret. You can open it at dinner.

BEULAH *(puts her arm around his neck and rubs her nose against his temple)* Crazy old pa, goin' buyin' things! It's me that oughta be buyin' things for you, Pa.

ELMER Oh, no! There's only one Loolie in the world.

BEULAH *(whispering, as her eyes fill with tears)* Are you glad I'm still alive, Pa?

*(She kisses him abruptly and goes back to the house steps.)*

ELMER Where's Horace, Loolie?

BEULAH He was kep' a little at the office. He'll be here any minute. He's crazy to see you all.

MA All right. You men go over to the Y and come back in about an hour.

BEULAH Go straight along, Pa, you can't miss it. It just stares at yuh. *(Elmer and Arthur exit down right.)* Well, come on upstairs, Ma, and take your things. – Caroline, there's a surprise for you in the back yard.

CAROLINE Rabbits?

BEULAH No.

CAROLINE Chickins?

BEULAH No. Go and see. *(Caroline runs off stage, down left.)* There are two new puppies. You be thinking over whether you can keep one in Newark.

MA I guess we can. *(Ma and Beulah turn and walk way up stage right. The Stage Manager pushes out a cot from the left, and places it down left on a slant so that its foot is toward the left. Beulah and Ma come down stage center toward left.)* It's a nice house, Beulah. You just got a lovely home.

BEULAH When I got back from the hospital, Horace had moved everything into it, and there wasn't anything for me to do.

MA It's lovely.

*(Beulah sits on the cot, testing the springs.)*

BEULAH I think you'll find this comfortable, Ma. *(Beulah sits on down stage end of it.)*

MA *(taking off her hat)* Oh, I could sleep on a heapa shoes, Loolie! I don't have no trouble sleepin'. *(She sits down up stage of her.)* Now let me look at my girl. Well, well, when I last saw you, you didn't know me. You kep' saying: *When's Mama comin'? When's Mama comin'?* But the doctor sent me away.

BEULAH *(puts her head on her mother's shoulder and weeps)* It was awful, Mama. It was awful. She didn't even live a few minutes, Mama. It was awful.

MA *(in a quick, light, urgent undertone)* God thought best, dear. God thought best. We don't understand why. We just go on, honey, doin' our business. *(Then almost abruptly.)* Well, now *(stands up),* what are we giving the men to eat tonight?

BEULAH There's a chicken in the oven.

MA What time didya put it in?

BEULAH *(restraining her)* Aw, Ma, don't go yet. *(Taking her mother's hand and drawing her down beside her.)* I like to sit here with you this way. You always get the fidgets when we try and pet yuh, Mama.

MA *(ruefully, laughing)* Yes, it's kinda foolish. I'm just an old Newark bag-a-bones.

*(She glances at the backs of her hands.)*

BEULAH *(indignantly)* Why, Ma, you're good-lookin'! We always said you were good-lookin'. – And besides, you're the best ma we could ever have.

MA *(uncomfortable)* Well, I hope you like me. There's nothin' like bein' liked by your family. – *(Rises.)* Now I'm going downstairs to look at the chicken. You stretch out here for a minute and shut your eyes. *(She helps Beulah to a lying position.)* Have you got everything laid in for breakfast before the shops close?

BEULAH Oh, you know! Ham and eggs.

*(They both laugh. Ma puts an imaginary blanket over Beulah.)*

MA I declare I never could understand what men see in ham and eggs. I think they're horrible. – What time did you put the chicken in?

BEULAH Five o'clock.

MA Well, now, you shut your eyes for ten minutes.

*(Ma turns, walks directly up stage, then along the back wall to the right as she absent-mindedly and indistinctly sings):*

There were ninety and nine that safely lay
In the shelter of the fold ...

*and the curtain falls*

## Biographical Notes

*Thornton Wilder was born in 1897 to parents who were both seriously religious: his father was a Congregationalist who insisted on Puritan virtues and his mother was the daughter of a Presbyterian minister. He was strongly influenced by their beliefs.*

*Wilder attended Oberlin College and then transferred to Yale. He contributed substantially to the literary magazine of each college, having by then found his true vocation. While on an archaeological dig in Italy, he participated in the unearthing of an Etruscan street, which deeply influenced him by making clear to him the larger context in which to view the human condition.*

*The attempt to view man's existence in a larger historical and philosophical framework found expression in his literary works, among them "Our Town" (1938), which won Wilder one of the three Pulitzer Prizes he was awarded in his lifetime. The radically bare stage of "Our Town", also found in "The Happy Journey", allows for a symbolism which makes the stage represent the world. In 1928 he won the Pulitzer Prize for his novel "The Bridge of San Luis Rey". Wilder's "The Skin of Our Teeth" won him his third Pulitzer in 1943. It is an imaginative and timeless recapitulation of the entire history of the human race, stressing man's ability to survive somehow, despite the destructive forces of Nature and man's own folly. "The Happy Journey to Trenton and Camden", which Wilder once singled out as his best play, comes from a collection of six one-acters entitled "The Long Christmas Dinner and Other Plays" (1931).*

*Even when working with the provincial, Wilder manages to reach beyond to the universal. He once wrote: "The human adventure is much the same in all times and all places."*

*Thornton Wilder died in 1975.*

## Annotations

**26** 8 **scenery** stage decoration – 9 **back-drop** background – 10 **cyclorama** [ˌsaɪk-lə'ræmə] a large pictorial representation encircling the spectator suggesting unlimited space – 11 **proscenium pillar** [prəʊ'si:njəm] a column providing support for the stage structure – 12 **marbles** *Murmeln* – 16 **I declare** *(coll.)* exclamation showing strongly held opinion – 20 **plagued** [pleɪgd] *(dial.)* troublesome – 23 **to mutter** to speak in a low and badly articulated manner – **reluctantly** [–'– – –] in a hesitant way, slowly – 25 **swiftly** quickly – 26 **to fling** to throw with force – **impact** forceful contact – 27 **aggie** ['ægɪ] a marble

**27** 1 **serenely** [sɪ'ri:nlɪ] calmly – 2 **hoodlum** ['hu:dləm] a rowdy or misbehaved person – 7 **consulting his script** looking at a typed-out version of the play – 11 **spat it up** coughed it up – 14 **grateful** ['greɪtfʊl] feeling or showing thanks – 18 **Beulah** ['bju:lə] from Hebrew, literally meaning married (said of a woman) – 23 **downright** *(sl.)* very – 25 **I ain't** *(sl.) here:* I haven't – **without I see her** *(dial.)* without seeing her – 37 **yuh** *(sl.)* = you

**28** 6 **vigorously** ['vɪgərəslɪ] energetically – 11 **musta** *(sl.)* = must have – 12 **mercy** blessing – **what you done** *(sl.)* what have you done – 14 **defiant-abashed** [dɪ'faɪənt ə'bæʃt] bold and ashamed – 21 **spectacles** glasses – **garage** *A.E.* [gə'rɑ:ʒ] – 23 **luggage** e.g. suitcases, *B.E.* baggage – 24 **I wouldn't like to have no** *(sl.)* I wouldn't like to have any – 30 **porch** a veranda, often in the back or in the front of houses – 31 **denote** [dɪ'nəʊt] *here:* to make it look like ...

**29** 2 **to shift gears** [gɪəz] *Gangschaltung betätigen, schalten* – 18 **tremendous** [trə'mendəs] very large – 20 **lurch** to move suddenly – 26 **nod** *nicken* – 28 **banquet** ['bænkwɪt] ceremonial or formal dinner – **Lodge** the meeting place of a fraternal organization

**30** 2 **graduation** *(Schul-)Abschluß* – 3 **gazing** looking – 4 **to whine** to complain like a child or a dog – **funeral** ['fju:nərəl] ceremony when s.o. has died – 6 **to crane forward** to stretch one's neck in order to see better – **absorbed** *here:* complete – 9 **banner** a kind of flag – **Elizabeth** town in New Jersey – 11 **solemn** ['sɒləm] serious – 26 **Rite** non-standard orthographic variant of *right* – **suspenders** [səs'pendəz] *Hosenträger* – 28 **Missy** diminuitive form of Miss *(kleines Fräulein)* – 29 **to tease** [ti:z] to make fun of s.o., to annoy s.o. – 33 **go along** *(dial.)* 'don't give me that'

**31** 2 **we aim to please** phrase often used in advertisements *(bei uns ist der Kunde König)* – 10 **leap year** the year in which February has 29 days – 18 **comfort station** euphemistic expression referring to public toilets – 19 **unruffled** [ʌn'rʌfld] not upset – 24 **yewman** = human – 26 **peaked** in bad shape, sickly – 27 **leavings** food remaining after a meal – **billboard** a flat surface, generally along roads and highways, on which advertisements are pasted – 32 **paper route** a particular territory in which newspapers are delivered to subscribers *(Abonnenten)*

**32** 3 **sullenly** *here:* disapprovingly – 5 **outraged** extremely angry – 13 **to spoil** to make unsatisfactory – 17 **to concede** [kən'si:d] to give in – 22 **speakeasy** a place where alcoholic drinks were illegally sold (during the years of Prohibition in the United States, 1919–1933) – 30 **garage hand** a person who works at a car repair shop – 31 **radiator** *Kühler* – 33 **to punch** to hit with the fist – 37 **to get fixed up** *(coll.)* to have s.th. checked

**33** 1 **hood** part of car covering engine – 7 **burg** *(A.E., coll.)* city, town – 10 **rung**

*Verstrebung, Sprosse* – 11 **to take a fancy to s.o.** to come to like s.o. very much – 14 **pokin'** = poking; to push s.o. with one's finger – 18 **Y.M.C.A.** *abbrev. for* Young Men's Christian Association – 19 **dormitory** ['dɔ:mɪtrɪ] a large room in which many people sleep – 21 **Knights of Columbus** a fraternal and benevolent society of Roman Catholic men – 23 **the Y** *short for* the Y.M.C.A. – 28 **to jolt** to make an abrupt movement – 33 **kinda** *(spoken language)* = kind of

**34** 8 **weed** *Unkraut* – 10 **the Union** the United States – 14 **cast down** depressed, troubled – 15 **falteringly** hesitatingly, reluctantly – 18 **wicked** ['wɪkɪd] evil – 19 **to weep** to cry – 23 **sakes alive** *(dial.)* an exclamation expressing surprise and/or impatience – 25 **beau** [bəʊ] *(French)* sweetheart, darling

**35** 6 **to survey** to take an inclusive, overall view of s.th. – **didactic** [daɪ'dæktɪk] in a manner appropriate to a teacher – 7 **duly** properly, appropriately – 10 **license** *(short for* "license plate"); metal plate on which a car's registration number is printed – 16 **a lotta** *(sl.)* = a lot of – 33 **liblong** *(dial.)* livelong, i.e. all day long

**36** 9 **sorta** *(informal)* = sort of, kind of – 22 **Longfellow,** Henry Wadsworth, American poet (1807–82) – 26 **grim** serious, stern – 30 **unmalicious mimicry** imitation which does not mean to harm or hurt

**37** 1 **laboriously** [lə'bɔ:rɪəslɪ] with great effort – 4 **A and P** (usually A & P; short for Atlantic and Pacific); U.S. grocery store chain – 5 **kitty-corner** *(coll.)* catty-cornered, diagonally across – **jubilantly** showing great delight, gladness – 12 **glassy** cold, hard – 15 **to glare** to look at s.o. in a severe way – 25 **affectionately** lovingly – 35 **temple** *Schläfe*

**38** 15 **puppy** small dog – 18 **cot** small portable bed *(Feldbett)* – 19 **slant** angle – 28 **heapa** *(sl.)* = heap of, pile of

**39** 4 **didya** *(sl.)* = did you – 5 **to restrain** to hold back – 7 **to get the fidgets** = to fidget; to become nervously, restlessly ill at ease (to fidget = *herumzappeln*) – 8 **rueful** ['ru:fʊl] pitiable, mournful, sad – **bag-a-bones** = bag of bones; a person who looks like he is suffering from hunger – 10 **to glance at** to look at – 11 **indignant** [–'– –] a manner expressive of (angry) disapproval – 26 **indistinctly** not clearly – 28 **fold** enclosure for sheep; *here:* group of people with the same religious belief/faith

# Interpretation and Teaching Notes

## Content and Analysis

The play opens with Ma Kirby, the *de facto* head of a lower middle-class Newark, New Jersey household, rounding up her two children and husband for a drive to Camden. They are going to visit her married daughter Beulah who has recently returned from the hospital where her baby died shortly after birth. Ma fusses over her thirteen-year-old son Arthur, insisting that he cannot come along unless he finds his hat. Ma makes arrangements with a neighbor, Mrs. Schwartz (played by the stage manager who reads from a script) to feed the cat while they are away. Ma explains to another neighbor, Mrs. Hobmeyer (also played by the stage manager) that they are using her husband Elmer's one-week yearly vacation from work to visit Beulah in Camden, located a short drive from Newark. She reveals that Beulah has been sick, as she puts it, and that she needs to visit her to see how she is doing. En route, the family is held up by a funeral procession, which annoys Caroline, the fifteen-year-old daughter, but which affords Ma the opportunity to philosophize, in her own fashion, and to suggest that the rest of her family think, as she herself does, about the significance of death. Her children are not enthusiastic about such sermonizing.

The journey resumes, and the family engage in light conversation until Arthur makes the mistake of mocking Ma's constant references to God. This brings the play to the first of its two dramatic climaxes. Ma, enraged, orders her husband to stop the car and declares that Arthur will have to return to Newark by himself as punishment for making fun of God. Elmer manages to calm his wife down, and they drive on, though burdened by a certain silence resulting from the "scandal." Elmer helps relieve the strained atmosphere by stopping at a gas station, which is attended by a nice young man (again played by the stage manager), with whom Ma seems to be getting on very well. They stop for hot dogs after leaving the gas station, and Arthur takes advantage of the opportunity to apologize to his mother for what he said. He and Caroline burst into tears, creating the second dramatic climax, because Ma once again emphasizes the seriousness of the sin committed against God. Ma, however, rising to the occasion, saves the situation and re-establishes harmony in the best motherly fashion. They complete their trip to Camden with talk and singing.

Beulah greets her family, and the "men-folk" are sent off to the Y.M.C.A., to return when the women have dinner on the table. Beulah, alone with her mother, is cut short by her when she begins to talk about how awful her hospital experience was. Ma, bringing the play to its thematic climax, invokes God as the omniscient arbiter of all things, telling Beulah that He has His reasons for what He does or allows to happen. Then she abruptly changes the subject. The play ends with Ma, after having covered her beloved Beulah with a blanket so she can nap, walking off absent-mindedly singing a hymn the text of which refers to the parable of the good shepherd.

*The Happy Journey to Trenton and Camden* (1931), Thornton Wilder's favorite play, and one that he subtitled *The Portrait of a Lady,*[1] focuses on a single character. This character, Ma Kirby, is portrayed in her familial environment, a thoroughly provincial and banal setting, with everything subordinated to the purpose of presenting her particular personality. Wilder carefully limits the other characters' actions and utterances so that, although they are not cardboard figures, they fail to reach the degree of well-roundedness that we find with Ma.

Ma is the kind of person who subscribes to a particular belief system which orders her life in the largest possible sense. She possesses a belief which eases "metaphysical anxiety", offers relief from the gnawing questions of the meaning of life by declaring the existence of an Almighty who is in control of and responsible for an ordered and meaningful cosmos. Wilder shows through his treatment of Ma the kind of comfort and strength a person can get by believing in such an explanation of life.

Wilder portrays this mentality and brings the play to its thematic climax when Ma declares "God thought best, dear ... We don't ask why. We just go on, honey, doin' our business" (**38** 36–**39** 1) in response to Beulah's anxious remarks about how awful it was to lose the baby. It is a mentality which raises all earthly events into a cosmic scheme, as it were. Even the most potentially disturbing of experiences – such as the death of a just delivered baby – fails to disrupt this kind of psychological balance. Ma has faith that the universe has order and purpose, even though that order and purpose may not be understandable to the individual. The play's conclusion supports this theme of a belief system:

> "There were ninety and nine that safely lay
> In the shelter of the fold ..."

1 Cf. Donald Haberman, *The Plays of Thornton Wilder. A Critical Study,* Middletown, Conn, 1967, p. 103.

The fact that she sings the lines of a hymn expressing her trust in God as the good shepherd "absent-mindedly" indicates how deeply ingrained this belief is.

Ma's belief in the existence of an all-powerful God truly governs her life. Not only does He give her an understanding (such as it is) of disturbing and painful experiences, but He also explains more positive ones. "God has done a lot of things for me and I won't have him be made fun of by anybody" (**32** 11–12). She then declares that it is due to her faith in God that her family managed to escape the sinfulness of frequenting "speakeasies and nightclubs."

Ma's is a world view which orders the cosmos and provides an explanation for everything, positive and negative. And yet, while making life easy in many respects, it is a belief which also involves responsibility, thus giving purpose to life in the here and now. Wilder's having her declare, "Well, I'm 'ready,' children. I hope everybody in this car is 'ready'" (**30** 18–19) represents the Christian emphasis on an individual's having to account for his or her earthly behavior at a final Day of Judgment. Believing in a religion which gives form and meaning to her existence, Ma gets the strength to operate in the here and now with character and authority.

Elmer is the model of the obedient husband (although Ma does let him make some decisions). When Arthur and Caroline burst into tears after Arthur is reminded of the wickedness of his remark, Ma capably takes hold of the situation and prevents it from turning into total chaos. She suddenly becomes "joyously alive and happy" (**34** 22–23). Intuitively she assumes a role that seems carefully calculated to stop the tension and tears that have resulted from the disruption of familial harmony. Momentarily carried away by the strength of her convictions ("We all say wicked things at times. I know you didn't mean it like it sounded" **34** 18–19), Ma causes the chaos in the first place, but quite capably saves the situation through clever parental manipulation. She does indeed represent "the management" in this household.

As the authority figure, she insists on moral correctness in the behavior of her children, which derives from her religion. Caroline's quick reply to Ma when she asks if they would like to hear her wishes – "you want me to be a good girl and you want Arthur to be honest-in-word-and-deed" (**36** 31–32) – shows this insistence on moral uprightness. Her preference for the popular belief that George Washington "never told a lie" (**35** 7) over the claim that he was "first in war and first in peace, and first in the hearts of his countrymen" (**35** 4–5) is another example of this. Her ready sermon delivered to Caroline when she makes the mistake of remarking upon the apparent material success of Beulah and her husband similarly represents her concern with moral correctness, but also reveals her love of her family:

> I don't want to hear anybody talking about rich or not rich when I'm around. If people aren't nice I don't care how rich they are. I live in the best street in the world because my husband and children live there. (**37** 12–15)

This is a rather trite thing to say, certainly; and yet, it represents something in which Ma truly believes (and one which is not without its merits). The fact that Wilder has Ma speak "dreamily but not sentimentally" (**30** 12) when she sermonizes about the significance of death indicates that he does not want to dismiss her as a fool. If what she proclaims seems trite, it is at least heartfelt.

Her insistence on the "rightness" of behavior in the here and now extends beyond moral matters. It seems as if it would be almost as scandalous to head off somewhere without a hat as it is to use the Lord's name disrespectfully. While offering Caroline the praiseworthy example of thinking relatively – "You do your way and I'll do mine" (**33** 33) – Ma is far from being the tolerant type suggested by such a statement. Evidence for this is found immediately after her enlightened declaration. In the very next breath she reveals cultural narrow-mindedness when she refers to "those dreadful Greek places" (**33** 35) which she imagines the station attendant frequents. Her generosity is undercut by her own words.

There is, however, a more serious criticism to be made of Ma than to observe that her ordered and harmonious world view is somewhat rigid and narrow-minded. Her belief system actually can be seen as denying her the opportunity to explore life in an honest, personal manner. Her way of thinking deprives her of any genuine understanding of the mystery of the human condition. Her belief in God gives form and meaning to her life. But she backs away from entering into larger experiences and questions because of her too easy invocation of God as the explanation of everything.

This inability to confront intellectually the more disturbing and tragic aspects of life leads Ma to a certain superficiality. Because she herself is unable to explore the significance of her daughter's baby dying at childbirth, she is uncomfortable discussing that fact with others. Hence her simple explanations to the neighbor and her children: "My married daughter was downright sick a while ago" (**27** 23); "Now, children, you be good and quiet during dinner. She's just got out of bed after a big sorta operation..." (**36** 8–9). Her reaction to Beulah's genuine display of emotion is very suggestive of this state of mind. Her response is "quick" and "urgent". Beulah has moved onto dangerous ground in talking about how awful the experience was, and must be cut short immediately before she says or reveals more. Ma's message ("God thought best, dear. God thought best...") assuages that "metaphysical anxiety", and is a counter to the urgent matter at hand. Unable to allow for further discussion, she uses that familiar technique of uttering a "well, now" accompanied by the appropriate body language (she stands up). Her "Well, now, what are we giving the men to eat tonight?" (**39** 1–2) signals to Beulah, who clearly needs to discuss the trauma she has gone through, that the talk about her terrible experience is over. This does not mean that Ma is incapable of sincere and heartfelt sympathy. Her way of comforting Beulah is simply to slip again into her role as mother and to tend to the physical well-being of her family.

While her intellectual capacity is severely limited, and her behavior as a result appears somewhat superficial, Ma is, as an individual human being, sufficiently happy and, as a mother, significantly successful. For all her limitations, she comes across as a character worthy of respect for what she does possess, for being what she is – as opposed to deserving criticism for what she is not. Wilder takes as his subject the personality and psychology of an ordinary human being. He portrays her realistically, showing her strengths as well as her weaknesses. Carefully considered, the characterization of Ma reveals neutrality on the part of the playwright. It seems fair to conclude that Wilder himself did not intend to criticize Ma for her shortcomings.

In fact, Wilder's comments on the play reveal that he viewed Ma Kirby in a rather favorable light. He once characterized *The Happy Journey* as "a testimonial of homage to the average American mother who brings up her children as instinctively as a bird builds its nest and whose strength lies in the fact that whatever stress arrives from the circumstances of life, she strives to maintain an atmosphere of forward looking industry and readiness."[2]

The play is light in tone and appears to offer nothing more than a look at a day in the life of a common American family. It is concerned only with provincialities and banalities which make up daily life almost everywhere. But behind this appearance of ordinariness lies a carefully considered and constructed presentation of something fundamental in terms of human personality types, accomplished through careful selection of detail with high compression. That Wilder achieves the characterization of a basic personality type from material full of references to such miscellaneous everyday

2 Quoted in Haberman, *op. cit.*, p. 104.

things as spaghetti, the A & P, comfort stations and the local Y.M.C.A. makes his accomplishment all the more remarkable. Wilder takes as his material the thoroughly pedestrian; he works through it, however, to arrive at something larger. As he indicates at the very beginning of *The Happy Journey to Trenton and Camden,* "the idea is that no place [in particular] is being represented."

## First Unit: The Stage and the Stage Language

In Wilder's plays, the fictitious quality of the stage reality is consciously made apparent by the innovative nature of the staging and by the introduction of the stage manager. The "empty, bare stage", the "imaginary mirror" make for a similarly detached and critical participation as Brecht's A-effects, enabling the audience to infer the general from the particular. The play does not need to be based on a meaningful plot but may consist of mere action, designed to represent everyday life in general, organized – sometimes even acted out – by the stage manager. The importance of Wilder's techniques for the understanding of his play in particular and modern drama in general, therefore, justifies an initially formalistic approach to the drama.

The students should have read the play up to **33** 28 beforehand, and have listed all the technical terms that have to do with scenery and staging.

1. *Describe the instructions the author gives in terms of props and characters. Describe the function of the stage manager.*
Wilder deliberately avoids references to a "real" time-space scheme by leaving the stage "bare". The actors have to rely on gestures and pantomime rather than props.

Besides the dramatis personae, there is the stage manager, who is "consulting his script" when slipping into the action, and who plays several roles, even female ones.

2. *What advantages do you see in this kind of theatrical scheme?*
The students' answers will of course depend on their individual appreciation, experience and knowledge. So the teacher may have to guide the discussion to some extent.
Parallels to Brecht or Pirandello, the Chinese and Japanese theater can be drawn in terms of non-identification, analytical observation and critical detachment. On the one hand, the general lack of illusion, of visual stimuli and of characters one can identify with – familiar theatrical devices, so to

speak – harbors the danger of boredom; on the other hand, it leaves room for one's own imagination, room to fill gaps in time and space. In addition, the pantomimical acting may result in humorous highlights.

Thornton Wilder once pointed out the superiority of certain stage conventions over pure realism:

> The history of the theatre shows us that in its greatest ages the stage employed the greatest number of conventions. The stage is fundamental pretense and it thrives on the acceptance of that fact and in the multiplication of additional pretenses. When it tries to assert that the personages in the action "really are", really inhabit such and such rooms, really suffer such and such emotions, it loses rather than gains credibility. (...)
> 1. It [stage convention] provokes the collaborative activity of the spectator's imagination; and
> 2. It raises the action from the specific to the general.[3]

About *The Happy Journey* he said that he "tried to capture not verisimilitude but reality".[4]

| **Staging** | **Effects** |
|---|---|
| • no classical theatrical devices such as scenery, props, stage sets | • no illusion is created |
| • a stage manager plays various roles; the emphasis is therefore drawn away from the minor characters and clearly concentrated on others | • the audience is distanced from the action; does not identify with the actors (A-effects), may arrive at something larger than the reality presented on stage |
| • when "consulting the manuscript", the stage manager is more a narrator than an actor (epic devices!) | |
| • the actors often rely on mime and gestures rather than on action (dramatic devices!) | • there is room for the audience to use their own imagination |
| • detailed stage directions are given | • the author gets his particular message across (didactic intention) |

---

3 Thornton Wilder, "Some Thoughts on Playwriting," in Horst Frenz, ed., *American Playwrights on Drama,* New York, 1965, pp. 59–60.

4 Thornton Wilder, "A Platform and a Passion or Two," in Horst Frenz, ed., *op. cit.*, p. 124.

**Homework**
Finish reading the play. Underline passages that reveal Ma Kirby's character.

## Second Unit: Ma Kirby

1. *Describe Ma Kirby's position in the family. Find suitable references in the text for your judgment.*
Ma is the "boss", the actual head of the family (though not the breadwinner) since she arranges and plans everything (cf. the opening scene).

She is the first and the last to speak in the play. The general mood of the family depends highly on her approving of the situation (cf. her reaction to Arthur's impertinence). She decides who wears or does what (e. g. **28** 15; **31** 23–25; **34** 24–32).

2. *What is Ma's world view like?*
Her world view is a religious one. The episode in which Arthur mockingly refers to his mother's correspondence with God (**32** 3–4) suggests how absolutely she believes in God. She is grateful to Him for all the good things in her life (**32** 11), and she is convinced that without proper respect for Him the family would be frequenting "speakeasies and nightclubs and places like that" (**32** 22–23). Furthermore, she is perfectly sure that God is in absolute control of things, omniscient and protective: "God thought best, dear. (...) We don't understand why" (**38** 36–37). Consequently, she shares the Christian conviction that one has to be "ready" for when one has "to go" (**30** 19), as everybody will have to account for their behavior.

3. *How would you characterize Ma Kirby?*
She is a friendly and motherly person who seems to get along well with her neighbors. Wilder himself points out that she is "sympathetic" and "mod-

est". One might say she behaves according to what is considered decent and conventional. She is strict with her children and domineering at times, but at other times she can be humorous. She is amazingly self-assured if not opinionated. Her statements are often superficial and commonplace. When one considers her references to "those awful Greek places" (they supposedly account for people's looking "pale" and badly fed) in the light of all-American hot-dog stands (which apparently serve sausages with inedible skin), her attitude could be qualified as culturally narrow-minded and prejudiced.

4. *How does Ma behave in the Beulah scene? What does Beulah expect of her?*
Beulah needs to talk about the trauma she has recently undergone. Grieved as she is, she expects her mother to listen to her; she needs sympathy and comfort, understanding and affection. But Ma does not listen: "In a quick, light, urgent undertone" (**38** 36) she eases the sorrow by telling her to rely on God's benevolence rather than her own ability to understand and explain. She is unable to explore the depth and significance of her daughter's misfortune.

She seems uncomfortable when admitting or even discussing the baby's death, which explains her evasive remarks earlier on when telling a neighbor about the reason for the journey (**27** 22–23) and when she implores Arthur and Caroline to be "good and quiet during dinner" (**36** 8).

It is not that Ma wants to withhold comfort and affection from her daughter, on the contrary, as becomes clear when we consider that she had visited her daughter before in the hospital (**38** 30–33). Being incapable of confronting her daughter's problem on an intellectual level, she has to resort to trust in God's wisdom and her own role as a mother who has to provide for the physical well-being of her family. Her remark "We just go on, honey, doin' our business" (**38** 37–**39** 1) may sound banal, but it somehow transcends her daughter's grief and expresses a simple but deep wisdom (see also Wilder's own characterization of this character, quoted above page 65). The play's ending thus serves as a summary of Ma's character: nothing really matters, nothing really disrupts her happy constitution as long as there is shelter and safety – her family and God.

5. *Explain the title of the play.*
In spite of the sad occasion, the journey is a happy one because it presents a family secure in its relationship of mutual love. This is true despite the minor rebellions on the part of Arthur, which eventually result in tearful harmony.

6. *Go through the play again and list all references to Ma's character.*

**Ma Kirby's character**

She is:
- friendly with her neighbors (opening scene)
- sympathetic (**27** 25)
- modest (**27** 17)
- conventional (**30** 7)
- strict (**28** 15; **35** 6)
- patriotic (**30** 14)
- self-assured (**29** 24–25; **37** 12–15)
- protective (**31** 34–36)
- humorous (**31** 1–2)
- somewhat narrow-minded, prejudiced (**33** 35)
- superficial (**33** 29; **37** 12–15)
- family-conscious (**35** 22–23; **37** 12–15)
- manipulative, domineering (**34** 18–30)

The references in brackets are meant to give examples, the list is by no means complete.

**Homework**
Written characterization of Ma Kirby *or* written summary of the play.

## Third Unit: The American Way

1. *What do we learn about the Kirbys' social and economic background? Also consider their language.*
Mr. Kirby works in a laundry. The family live in a relatively poor neighborhood (cf. Caroline marveling at Beulah's street, which appears to her better than theirs; **37** 10). Instead of taking a room in a hotel, Mr. Kirby and Arthur stay in the Y.M.C.A., by far the cheapest accommodation available. The family's language is characterized by minor deviations from the standard (e.g. "without I see her", **27** 26; "drive careful", **31** 16; and cf. the stage direction "'route' rhymes with 'out'", **31** 32). Both their economic background and their language mark the Kirbys as thoroughly lower middle class.

2. *What do we learn about their cultural tastes?*
While driving through New Jersey the family visibly enjoy that much-maligned art form, the advertising billboard along the highway (cf. **30** 26–**31** 4; **31** 27–29). The skillful use of an advertising jingle on the part of Ma provokes laughter among the children and even brings a smile to the husband's face. Ma's admiration for a cigarette advertisement shows a certain

self-contradictory trait which, however, adds to her overall credibility as a character. We may safely assume that she would strongly disapprove if her daughter did smoke; this does not prevent her, however, from marveling at a woman who "looks like Beulah" in the advertisement.
The family's taste in art, then, is again lower middle class, but at the same time reveals a thorough enjoyment of America. (Note: Since the late 1960s the billboard has disappeared from most of America's highways).

3. *Schisgal's play has made us acquainted with the American Dream of Success; what is Ma's attitude towards this dream?*
Material success to Ma is less important than a lot of other things, her son's health for one, as her reaction to Arthur's suggestion that he would like to take on a new paper route shows (**31** 34–37). Though her refusal is again based on her religious beliefs (cf. **32** 1–2), it seems to have another dimension. When Caroline speculates on the relative wealth of Beulah and the people in her street, Ma refuses to enter into such a discussion. "Rich or not rich" (**37** 13) are categories which do not hold any significance in her world. Ma has a basically egalitarian attitude.

4. *What is the family's attitude toward other people?*
Ma's exclamation after the conversation with the gas station attendant (who, it should be noted, is the epitome of friendliness, although he does not make a cent when he services the Kirbys' car) is characteristic of her and the entire family's attitude toward others: "The world's full of nice people" (**33** 29). Friendly relations with her neighbors, respect for the dead, no matter where, human solidarity and a general atmosphere of good feeling are typical of her. Her apparent narrow-mindedness when she speaks of "those dreadful Greek places" (**33** 35) is just a minor flaw in an otherwise clean record.

5. *Considering the above questions and Ma's religiousness, what might Thornton Wilder's intention have been in writing the play?*
The play is a celebration of the American middle class and of democracy in general. As one critic has pointed out, Wilder wanted to "affirm the presence of universal religious and moral values in the everyday lives of Americans."[5] He does so without idealizing the American middle class, as Ma's inconsistencies, her prejudices and her bossiness show.
The play thus becomes a monument to the American way as the following passage may suggest:

---

5 Rex Burbank, *Thornton Wilder,* New York, 1961, p. 66.

ELMER: There are a hundred and twenty-six million [people in the U.S.], Kate.
MA (...): And they all like to drive out in the evening with their children beside 'em. Why doesn't somebody sing something? (**35** 21–24)

## For Further Study and Discussion

1. If you wanted to make this very American play more German, what alterations would you suggest?

2. Where does the name Beulah come from and what does it connote?
It comes from the Bible (Isaiah 62,4) and means, in Hebrew, "married". "It signifies the state in which the soul is 'married' to God, in a state of perfect assurance" (Christopher Gillie, *Longman Companion to English Literature)*.

3. As no props are required, the students should be able to perform parts of the play in class. We suggest that the same scene (e. g. the funeral scene) be prepared by different groups of students. Then the level of sympathy toward the protagonist, which can be deduced from the interpretation underlying the performance, can be compared and discussed.

4. Comparative reading: Read the introductory monologue of the Stage Manager in Wilder's *Our Town* (1938) and explain its function.

Tennessee Williams

# The Last of My Solid Gold Watches

This play is inscribed to Mr. Sidney Greenstreet, for whom the principal character was hopefully conceived.

Characters

MR. CHARLIE COLTON

A NEGRO, *a porter in the hotel*

HARPER, *a traveling salesman*

Scene

*A hotel room in a Mississippi Delta town. The room has looked the same, with some deterioration, for thirty or forty years. The walls are mustard-colored. There are two windows with dull green blinds, torn slightly, a ceiling-fan, a white iron bed with a pink counterpane, a washstand with rose-buds painted on the pitcher and bowl, and on the wall a colored lithograph of blindfolded Hope with her broken lyre.*

*The door opens and Mr. Charlie Colton comes in. He is a legendary character, seventy-eight years old but still "going strong." He is lavish of flesh, superbly massive and with a kingly dignity of bearing. Once he moved with a tidal ease and power. Now he puffs and rumbles; when no one is looking he clasps his hand to his chest and cocks his head to the warning heart inside him. His huge expanse of chest and belly is criss-crossed by multiple gold chains with various little fobs and trinkets suspended from them. On the back of his head is a derby and in his mouth a cigar. This is "Mistuh Charlie" – who sadly but proudly refers to himself as "the last of the Delta drummers." He is followed into the room by a Negro porter, as old as he is – thin and toothless and grizzled. He totes the long orange leather sample cases containing the shoes which Mr. Charlie is selling. He sets them down at the foot of the bed as Mr. Charlie fishes in his pocket for a quarter.*

MR. CHARLIE *(handing the coin to the Negro)* Hyunh!

NEGRO *(breathlessly)* Thankyseh!

MR. CHARLIE Huh! You're too old a darkey to tote them big heavy cases.

NEGRO *(grinning sadly)* Don't say that, Mistuh Charlie.

MR. CHARLIE I reckon you'll keep right at it until yuh drop some day.

NEGRO That's right, Mistuh Charlie. *(Mr. Charlie fishes in his pocket for another quarter and tosses it to the Negro, who crouches and cackles as he receives it.)*

MR. CHARLIE Hyunh!

NEGRO Thankyseh, thankyseh!

MR. CHARLIE Now set that fan in motion an' bring me in some ice-water by an' by!

NEGRO De fan don' work, Mistuh Charlie.

MR. CHARLIE Huh! Deterioration! Everything's going downhill around here lately!

NEGRO Yes, suh, dat's de troof, Mistuh Charlie, ev'ything's goin' downhill.

MR. CHARLIE Who all's registered here of my acquaintance? Any ole-timers in town?

NEGRO Naw, suh, Mistuh Charlie.

MR. CHARLIE "Naw-suh-Mistuh-Charlie" 's all I get any more! You mean to say I won't be able to scare up a poker-game?

NEGRO *(chuckling sadly)* Mistuh Charlie, you's de bes' judge about dat!

MR. CHARLIE Well, it's mighty slim pickin's these days. Ev'ry time I come in a town there's less of the old and more of the new and by God, nigguh, this new stand of cotton I see around the Delta's not worth pickin' off th' ground! Go down there an' tell that young fellow, Mr. Bob Harper, to drop up here for a drink!

NEGRO *(withdrawing)* Yes, suh.

MR. CHARLIE It looks like otherwise I'd be playin' solitaire!

*(The Negro closes the door. Mr. Charlie crosses to the window and raises the blind. The evening is turning faintly blue. He sighs and opens his valise to remove a quart of whisky and some decks of cards which he slaps down on the table. He pauses and clasps his hand over his chest.)*

MR. CHARLIE *(ominously to himself)* Boom-boom-boom-boom-boom! Here comes th' parade! *(After some moments there comes a rap at the door.)* Come awn in! *(Harper, a salesman of thirty-five, enters. He has never known the "great days of the road" and there is no vestige of grandeur in his manner. He is lean and sallow and has a book of colored comics stuffed in his coat pocket.)*

HARPER How is the ole war-horse?

MR. CHARLIE *(heartily)* Migthy fine an' dandy! How's the young squirrel?

HARPER Okay.

MR. CHARLIE That's the right answer! Step on in an' pour you'self a drink! Cigar?

HARPER *(accepting both)* Thanks, Charlie.

MR. CHARLIE *(staring at his back with distaste)* Why do you carry them comic sheets around with yuh?

HARPER Gives me a couple of laughs ev'ry once and a while.

MR. CHARLIE Poverty of imagination! *(Harper laughs a little resentfully.)* You can't tell me there's any real amusement in them things. *(He pulls it out of Harper's coat pocket.)* "Superman," "The Adventures of Tom Tyler!" Huh! None of it's half as fantastic as life itself! When you arrive at my age – which is seventy-eight – you have a perspective of time on earth that astounds you! Literally astounds you! Naw, you say it's not true, all of that couldn't have happened! And for what *reason?* Naw! You begin to wonder. ... Well ... You're with Schultz and Werner?

HARPER That's right, Charlie.

MR. CHARLIE That concern's a comparatively new one.

HARPER I don't know about that. They been in th' bus'ness fo' goin' on twenty-five years now, Charlie.

MR. CHARLIE Infancy! Infancy! You heard this one, Bob? A child in its infancy don't have half as much fun as adults – in their adultery! *(He roars with laughter. Harper grins. Mr. Charlie falls silent abruptly. He would have appreciated a more profound response. He remembers the time when a joke of his would precipitate a tornado. He fills up Harper's glass with whisky.)*

HARPER Ain't you drinkin'?

MR. CHARLIE Naw, suh. Quit!

HARPER How come?

MR. CHARLIE Stomach! Perforated!

HARPER Ulcers? *(Mr. Charlie grunts. He bends with difficulty and heaves a sample case onto the bed.)* I had ulcers once.

MR. CHARLIE *Ev'ry* drinkin' man has ulcers once. Some *twice.*

HARPER You've fallen off some, ain't you?

MR. CHARLIE *(opening the sample case)* Twenty-seven pounds I lost since August. *(Harper whistles. Mr. Charlie is fishing among his samples.)* Yay-*ep!* Twenty-seven pounds I lost since August. *(He pulls out an oxford which he regards disdainfully.)* Hmmm ... a waste of cow-hide! *(He throws it back in and continues fishing.)* A man of my age an' constitution, Bob – he oughtn't to carry so much of that – adipose tissue! It's – *(He straightens up, red in the face and puffing.)* – a terrible strain –

on the *heart!* Hand me that other sample – over yonder. I wan' t' show you a little eyeful of queenly footwear in our new spring line! Some people say that the Cosmopolitan's not abreast of the times! That is an allegation which I deny and which I intend to disprove by the simple display of one little calf-skin slipper! *(opening up the second case)* Here we are, Son! *(fishing among the samples)* You knew ole "Marblehead" Langner in Friar's Point, Mississippi.

HARPER Ole "Marblehead" Langner? Sure.

MR. CHARLIE They found him dead in his bath-tub a week ago Satiddy night. *Here's* what I'm lookin' faw!

HARPER "Marblehead"? Dead?

MR. CHARLIE *Buried!* Had a Masonic funeral. I helped carry th' casket. Bob, I want you t' look at this Cuban-heel, shawl-tongue, perforated toe, calf-skin Misses' sport-oxford! *(He elevates it worshipfully.)* I want you to look at this shoe – and tell me what you think of it in plain language! *(Harper whistles and bugs his eyes.)* Ain't that a piece of *real* merchandise, you squirrel? Well, suh, I want you t' know –!

HARPER Charlie, that certainly is a piece of merchandise there!

MR. CHARLIE Bob, that piece of merchandise is only a small indication – of what our spring line consists of! You don't have to pick up a piece of merchandise like that – with I.S.C. branded on it! – and examine it with the microscope t' find out if it's quality stuff as well as quality *looks!* This ain't a shoe that Mrs. Jones of Hattiesburg, Mississippi, is going to throw back in your face a couple or three weeks later because it come to pieces like *card*-board in th' first *rain!* No, suh – I want you to know! We got some pretty fast-movers in our spring line – I'm layin' my samples out down there in th' lobby first thing in th' mornin' – I'll pack 'em up an' be gone out of town by *noon* – But by the Almighty Jehovah I bet you I'll have to *wire* the office to mail me a bunch of *brand*-new order-books at my next stopping-*off* place, Bob! *Hot* cakes! *That's* what I'm sellin'! *(He returns exhaustedly to the sample case and tosses the shoe back in, somewhat disheartened by Harper's vaguely benevolent contemplation of the brass light-fixture. He remembers a time when people's attention could be more securely riveted by talk. He slams the case shut and glances irritably at Harper who is staring very sadly at the brown carpet.)* Well, suh – *(He pours a shot of whisky.)* It was a mighty shocking piece of news I received this afternoon.

HARPER *(blowing a smoke ring)* What piece of news was that?

MR. CHARLIE The news about ole Gus Hamma – one of the old war-horses from *way* back, Bob. He and me an' this boy's daddy, C. C., used t' play poker ev'ry time we hit town together in this here self-same room! Well, suh, I want you t' know –

HARPER *(screwing up his forehead)* I think I heard about that. Didn't he have a stroke or something a few months ago?

MR. CHARLIE He *did.* An' partly *recovered.*

HARPER Yeah? Last I heard he had t' be fed with a spoon.

MR. CHARLIE *(quickly)* He did an' he partly recovered! He's been goin' round, y'know, in one of them chairs with a 'lectric motor on it. Goes chug-chug-chuggin' along th' road with th' butt of a cigar in his mouth. Well, suh, yestuddy in Blue Mountain, as I go out the Elks' Club door I pass him comin' in, bein' helped by th' nigguh – "Hello! Hiyuh, Gus!" That was at six-fifteen. Just half an hour later Carter Bowman stepped inside the hotel lobby where I was packin' up my sample cases an' give me the information that ole Gus Hamma had just now burnt himself to death in the Elks' Club lounge!

HARPER *(involuntarily grinning)* What uh yuh talkin' about?

MR. CHARLIE Yes, suh, the ole war-horse had fallen asleep with that nickel cigar in his mouth – set his clothes on fire – and burnt himself right up like a piece of paper!

HARPER I don't believe yuh!

MR. CHARLIE Now, why on earth would I be lyin' to yuh about a thing like that? He burnt himself right up like a piece of paper!

HARPER Well, ain't that a bitch of a way for a man to go?

MR. CHARLIE *One* way – *another* way –! *(gravely)* Maybe you don't *know* it – but all of us ole-timers, Bob, are disappearin' *fast!* We all gotta quit th' road one time or another. Me, I reckon I'm pretty nearly the last of th' Delta drummers!

HARPER *(restively squirming and glancing at his watch)* The last – of th' Delta drummers! How long you been on th' road?

MR. CHARLIE Fawty-six yeahs in Mahch!

HARPER I don't believe yuh.

MR. CHARLIE Why would I tell you a lie about something like that? No, suh, I want you t' know – I want you t' know – Hmmm. ... I lost a mighty good customer this week.

HARPER *(with total disinterest, adjusting the crotch of his trousers)* How's that, Charlie?

MR. CHARLIE *(grimly)* Ole Ben Summers – Friar's Point, Mississippi ... Fell over dead like a bolt of lightning had struck him just as he went to pour himself a drink at the Cotton Planters' Cotillion!

HARPER Ain't that terrible, though! What was the trouble?

MR. CHARLIE Mortality, that was the trouble! Some people think that millions now living are never going to *die.* I don't think that – I think it's a misapprehension not borne out by the facts! We go like flies when we come to the end of the summer ... And who is going to prevent it? *(He becomes depressed.)* Who – is going – to prevent it! *(He nods gravely.)* The road is changed. The shoe industry is changed. These times are – revolution! *(He rises and moves to the window.)* I don't like the way that it looks. You can take it from me – the world that I used to know – the world that this boy's father used t' know – the world we belonged to, us old time war-horses! – is slipping and sliding away from under our shoes. Who is going to prevent it? The ALL-LEATHER slogan don't sell shoes any more. The stuff that a shoe's made of is not what's going to sell it any more! No! STYLE! SMARTNESS! APPEARANCE! That's what counts with the modern shoe-purchaser, Bob! But try an' tell your style department that. Why, I remember the time when all I had to do was lay out my samples down there in the lobby. Open up my order-book an' write out orders until my fingers *ached!* A *sales*-talk was not *necessary.* A store was a place where people sold merchandise and to sell merchandise the retail-dealer had to obtain it from the wholesale manufacturer, Bob! Where they get merchandise now I do not pretend to know. But it don't look like they buy it from wholesale dealers! Out of the air – I guess it materializes! Or maybe stores don't *sell* stuff any more! Maybe I'm living in a world of illusion! I recognize that possibility, too!

HARPER *(casually, removing the comic paper from his pocket)* Yep – yep. You must have witnessed some changes.

MR. CHARLIE Changes? A mild expression. Young man – I have witnessed – a REVOLUTION! *(Harper has opened his comic paper but Mr. Charlie doesn't notice, for now his peroration is really addressed to himself.)* Yes, a *revolution!* The atmosphere that I *breathe* is not the same! Ah, well – I'm an old war-horse. *(He opens his coat and lifts the multiple golden chains from his vest. An amazing number of watches rise into view. Softly, proudly he speaks.)* Looky here, young fellow! You ever seen a man with this many watches? How did I *acquire* this many time-pieces? *(Harper has seen them before. He glances above the comic sheet with affected amazement.)* At every one of the annual sales conventions of the Cosmopolitan Shoe Company in St. Louis a seventeen-jewel, solid-gold, Swiss-movement Hamilton watch is presented to the ranking salesman of the year! Fifteen of those watches have been awarded to me! I think that represents something! I think that's *something* in the way of achievement! ... Don't *you?*

HARPER Yes, *siree!* You bet I *do,* Mistuh Charlie! *(He chuckles at a remark in the comic sheet. Mr. Charlie sticks out his lips with a grunt of disgust and snatches the comic sheet from the young man's hands.)*

MR. CHARLIE Young man – I'm talkin' to *you,* I'm talkin' for your *benefit.* And I expect the courtesy of your attention until I am through! I may be an old war-horse. I may have received – the last of my solid gold watches ... But just the same – good manners are still a part of the road's tradition. And part of the *South's* tradition. Only a young peckerwood would look at the comics when old Charlie Colton is talking.

HARPER *(taking another drink)* Excuse me, Charlie. I got a lot on my mind. I got some business to attend to directly.

MR. CHARLIE And directly you shall attend to it! I just want you to know what I think of this new world of yours! I'm not one of those that go howling about a Communist being stuck in the White House now! I don't say that Washington's been took over by Reds! I don't say all of the wealth of the country is in the hands of the Jews! I like the Jews and I'm a friend to the niggers! I *do* say *this* – however. .... The world I knew is gone – gone – gone with the wind! My pockets are full of watches which tell me that my time's just about over! *(A look of great trouble and bewilderment appears on his massive face. The rather noble tone of his speech slackens into a senile complaint.)* All of them – pigs that was slaughtered – carcasses dumped in the river! Farmers receivin' payment *not* t' grow wheat an' corn an' *not* t' plant cotton! All of these alphabet letters that's sprung up all about me! Meaning – unknown – to men of my generation! The rudeness – the lack of respect – the newspapers full of strange items! The terrible – fast – dark – rush of events in the world! Toward what and where and why! ... I don't pretend to have any knowledge of now! I only say – and I say this very humbly – I don't understand – what's happened. ... I'm one of them monsters you see reproduced in museums – out of the dark old ages – the giant *rep*-tiles, and the dino-whatever-you-call-ems. BUT – I *do* know *this!* And I state it without any shame! Initiative – self-reliance – independence of character! The old sterling qualities that distinguished one man from another – the clay from the potters – the potters from the clay – are *(kneading the air with his hands)* How is it the old song goes? ... Gone with the roses of *yesterday!* Yes – with the *wind!*

HARPER *(whose boredom has increased by leaps and bounds)* You old-timers make one mistake. You only read one side of the vital statistics.

MR. CHARLIE *(stung)* What do you mean by that?

HARPER In the papers they print people *dead* in one corner and people *born* in the next and usually *one* just about levels *off* with the *other*.

MR. CHARLIE Thank you for that information. I happen to be the godfather of several new infants in various points on the road. However, I think you have missed the whole point of what I was saying.

HARPER I don't think so, Mr. Charlie.

MR. CHARLIE Oh, yes, you have, young fellow. My point is this: the ALL-LEATHER slogan is not what sells any more – not in shoes and not in humanity, neither! The emphasis isn't on quality. Production, production, yes! But out of inferior goods! *Ersatz* – that's what they're making 'em out of!

HARPER *(getting up)* That's your opinion because you belong to the past.

MR. CHARLIE *(furiously)* A piece of impertinence, young man! I expect to be accorded a certain amount of respect by whippersnappers like you!

HARPER Hold on, Charlie.

MR. CHARLIE I belong to – tradition. I am a *legend*. Known from one end of the Delta to the other. From the Peabody hotel in Memphis to Cat-Fish Row in Vicksburg. Mistuh Charlie – *Mistuh Charlie!* Who knows *you?* What do *you* represent? A line of goods of doubtful value, some kike concern in the East! Get out of my room! I'd rather play solitaire, than poker with men who're no more solid characters than the jacks in the deck! *(He opens the door for the young salesman who shrugs and steps out with alacrity. Then he slams the door shut and breathes heavily. The Negro enters with a pitcher of ice water.)*

NEGRO *(grinning)* What you shoutin' about, Mistuh Charlie?

MR. CHARLIE I lose my patience sometimes. Nigger –

NEGRO Yes, suh?

MR. CHARLIE You remember the way it used to be.

NEGRO *(gently)* Yes, suh.

MR. CHARLIE I used to come in town like a conquering hero! Why, my God, nigger – they all but laid red carpets at my feet! Isn't that so?

NEGRO That's so, Mistuh Charlie.

MR. CHARLIE This room was like a *throne*-room. My samples laid out over there on green velvet cloth! The ceiling-fan *going* – now *broken!* And over here – the wash-bowl an' pitcher removed and the table-top *loaded* with *liquor!* In and out from the time I arrived till the time I left, the men of the road who knew me, to whom I stood for things commanding respect! Poker – continuous! Shouting, laughing – hilarity! Where have they all gone to?

NEGRO *(solemnly nodding)* The graveyard is crowded with folks we knew, Mistuh Charlie. It's mighty late in the day!

MR. CHARLIE Huh! *(He crosses to the window.)* Nigguh, it ain't even late in the day any more – *(He throws up the blind.)* It's NIGHT! *(The space of the window is black.)*

NEGRO *(softly, with a wise old smile)* Yes, suh ... *Night,* Mistuh Charlie!

*Curtain*

## Biographical Notes

*Tennessee Williams was one of America's greatest dramatists, having influenced with his many plays not only the theater of his own country, but the international stage as well. Tennessee Williams was not so much a writer of the intellect as he was a dramatist of the emotions. He managed to evoke feeling and mood in his plays with great understanding.*

*Not surprisingly for a man who declared that writing was his reason for living, elements of Williams' private life found their way into his artistic creations. Born in Mississippi in 1911 to a very religious mother and a materialistic father, Williams grew up with contradictory impulses in his soul. They later manifested themselves in his writing.*

*After studying at various universities he wandered for several years, experiencing life at the lower realms of society. We see in his writing a remarkable sympathy for the misfit, the outcast, the down-and-out. They are portrayed as being caught in an unfriendly and hostile world.*

*"The Last of My Solid Gold Watches" comes from a volume of one-act plays published in 1946. His most famous plays, which were met with critical acclaim and financial success, are "The Glass Menagerie" (1945), "A Streetcar Named Desire" (1947) and "Cat on a Hot Tin Roof" (1955).*

*Suffering acutely in the 1960s from personal problems and a dependency on alcohol and pills, Williams experienced a psychological breakdown in 1969 and had to be institutionalized. But he continued to write plays. Tennessee Williams died in 1983.*

## Annotations

**43** 9 **deterioration** [dɪˌtɪərɪə'reɪʃn] worsening of quality – 10 **blind** a window-shade – 11 **counterpane** cloth cover for a bed – 12 **pitcher** large jug – 13 **blindfolded** with a cover over the eyes – **lyre** ['laɪə] harp-like instrument used by the ancient Greeks – 15 **lavish** ['lævɪʃ] having a lot of – 16 **superbly** [sju:'pɜ:blɪ] **massive** *here:* noble, lordly, majestic – **bearing** behaviour and appearance – 17 **tidal** ['taɪdəl] like an ocean wave – **puffs and rumbles** breathes quickly and makes a deep sound – 18 **to clasp** to hold tightly – **to cock** to turn, indicating attention – 19 **expanse** wide area – **to crisscross** to mark with lines which cross one another – 20 **fob** ornament attached to a watch chain – **trinket** ['trɪŋkɪt] ornament or jewel of little value – 21 **suspended** hanging – **derby** *(A.E.)* bowler hat – 23 **drummer** *(chiefly A.E.)* s.o. who travels about selling goods – 24 **grizzled** grey-haired – **to tote** [təʊt] *(coll.)* to carry – 27 **a quarter** a twenty-five-cent coin – 28 **hyunh!** = here you are (one of several attempts to represent the way people actually speak) – 29 **thankyseh!** = thank you, sir! – 30 **darkey** *(coll.)* black man (not polite)

**44** 2 **to reckon** *here:* to be of the opinion that – **to drop** *short for:* to drop dead – 4 **to crouch** [kraʊtʃ] to bend down – **to cackle** to laugh noisily, like a hen – 8 **by an' by** later on – 10 **de fan don' work** *(the porter's speech imitates the Southern black dialect)* = the fan does not work – 13 **dat's de troof** = that's the truth – 19 **to scare up** *here:* to cause to happen – 20 **to chuckle** to laugh gently – 21 **it's mighty slim pickin's** *(coll.)* there isn't much to choose from – 23 **stand** *here:* growth of plants – 26 **to withdraw** to leave – 27 **solitaire** ['sɒlɪteə] card-game for one player – 29 **valise** [və'li:z] *(A.E.)* small leather bag – 30 **deck** *here:* set – 32 **ominously** ['ɒmɪnəslɪ] in a manner indicating s.th. bad is about to happen – 33 **rap** knock – 35 **vestige** ['vestɪdʒ] trace or sign – 36 **lean and sallow** thin and with an unhealthy yellow color – 39 **fine and dandy!** *(coll.)* very good

**45** 5 **distaste** dislike, aversion – 8 **resentfully** not liking s.th. – 13 **to astound** to overwhelm with surprise – 18 **for going on** *(coll.)* for about – 21 **adultery** *Ehebruch* – 22 **he would have appreciated** he would have liked – 23 **more profound** *here:* stronger – 24 **to precipitate a tornado** *here:* to result in a storm (of laughter) – 30 **ulcer** open sore usually in the stomach – **to grunt** to make a sound in an unclear manner – **to heave** to lift with difficulty – 37 **oxford** low shoe – 39 **adipose** ['ædɪpəʊs] fatty

**46** 1 **over yonder** *(coll.)* over there – 3 **to be abreast of the times** to keep up with the times – 4 **allegation** charge, accusation – 12 **Masonic** [mə'sɒnɪk] from Mason or Freemason: a member of a secret all-male society – **casket** box in which one is buried – 13 **Cuban-heel** (... indicates fancy shoes) –

14 **elevates it worshipfully** lifts it up with great respect – 16 **bugs his eyes** opens his eyes very wide – **merchandise** ['mɜ:tʃəndaɪz] s.th. to be sold – 21 **branded** printed – 25 **cardboard** very heavy paper – 30 **hot cakes** (from the expression, "selling like hot cakes": selling extremely well) – 31 **exhausted** very tired – **to toss** to throw – 32 **disheartened** discouraged – **vaguely benevolent ...** [bɪ'nevələnt] (Harper is stupidly absorbed in an object, wholly unaware of Charlie) – 34 **riveted** ['rɪvɪtɪd] strongly held – **glances irritably** ['– – – –] looks in an annoyed way

**47** 3 **to screw up one's forehead** to frown – 9 **butt** end – 10 **the Elks** fraternal organization that supports various charities – 16 **involuntarily** done without intention – 17 **nickel** five-cent coin; costing five cents – 23 **ain't that a bitch ...?** *(sl.)* isn't that a terrible way to die? – 24 **gravely** seriously – 28 **restively squirming** ['skwɜ:mɪŋ] impatiently moving about – 35 **crotch** the place between a person's legs – 37 **grimly** sternly, seriously – 39 **cotillion** [kə'tɪljən] a formal ball

**48** 1 **mortality** *Sterblichkeit* – 3 **misapprehension** incorrect idea which is not proved by fact – 5 **grave** earnest, solemn – 19 **retail dealer ... wholesale manufacturer** *Einzelhändler ... Großhändler, Hersteller* – 24 **casually** ['kæʒjʊəlɪ] in a careless way – 25 **to witness** to see – 28 **peroration** [ˌperə'reɪʃn] *here:* lengthy speech – 34 **timepiece** watch, clock – 35 **affected** pretended, not genuine – 37 **ranking** of highest rank, e.g. most successful

**49** 3 **disgust** strong disapproval – 4 **benefit** good – 5 **courtesy** ['kɜ:tɪsɪ] politeness – 8 **peckerwood** poor Southern white person – 14 **Communist ... in the White House** opponents of Franklin D. Roosevelt (American president 1933–45) accused him of being a communist – 20 **bewilderment** state of being confused – 21 **to slacken** to become slower, less active – 22 **to slaughter** ['slɔ:tə] to kill – **carcass** ['kɑ:kəs] dead body of an animal – 23 **alphabet letters** reference to the government agencies created by President Roosevelt to lead the country out of the depression; the agencies were referred to by abbreviations – 32 **self-reliance** confidence in one's own efforts – 33 **sterling** having the highest standard – **clay** a kind of earth – 34 **potter** person who makes articles out of clay – **to knead** [ni:d] to work on material (flour, clay, etc.) with the hands – 37 **by leaps and bounds** immensely, quickly – 40 **to sting** *here:* to cause s.o. sharp pain with words

**50** 13 **furiously** angrily – **impertinence** *Unverschämtheit* – **to accord** to give – 14 **whippersnapper** a (young) person who is too bold and self-confident – 21 **kike** *(sl.)* Jew *(derogatory)* – 22 **jack** a playing card *(Bube)* – 23 **to shrug** to raise the shoulders in a manner indicating doubt, indifference – 24 **alacrity** [ə'lækrətɪ] cheerful willingness – 35 **velvet** *Samt* – 38 **to command** *here:* to deserve and get – 39 **hilarity** [hɪ'lærɪtɪ] loud laughter

# Interpretation and Teaching Notes

## Content and Analysis

Mr. Charlie Colton, a massive and majestic seventy-eight-year-old man, enters a Mississippi Delta hotel room which has remained the same for several decades, except for a few signs of deterioration. Charlie, like the room, has seen better days. His heart is showing signs of wear and tear, and he is upset about the fact that the world is not what it used to be. But at the same time he is proud of his accomplishments as a once-successful shoe salesman who has received fifteen solid gold watches – awards for his good salesmanship.

Tipping the old black porter, Charlie suggests that the black man will probably keep working until he drops dead. A broken fan causes Charlie to declare that everything is falling apart; and he laments the fact that every time he passes through a town he finds "less of the old and more of the new". Outside it is getting dark.

Informed by the black porter that none of his old-time companions are registered in the hotel, Mr. Charlie settles for the second best and invites Bob Harper, a younger shoe salesman, to come up for a drink. Charlie himself has given up drinking because of his failing health.

The remainder of the play consists of the conversation between Charlie and Harper, which, for the greater part may be more properly termed a monologue.

Harper is an unwilling audience, possibly following Charlie's invitation out of a remnant of respect for the "old war-horse" and lured by the prospect of a free drink and cigar. During the conversation he is all but made responsible for the changes that Charlie is unable to understand in "this new world of yours" (**49** 13). Charlie starts out by ridiculing Harper for reading comics ("Poverty of imagination!" **45** 8) and tries to impress the younger man with his age and experience by calling Harper's company, Schultz and Werner (note the foreign names) – though in business for a quarter of a century – comparatively young, in fact a company in its "infancy". Looking at his own samples, he dismisses one of them as worthless and points to another as the epitome of value.

He tries to win the attention of a bored Harper by telling him about the recent deaths of old friends of his, "Marblehead" Langner, who was found dead in his bathtub; or Gus Hamma, who went up in flames after falling asleep in his wheelchair with a cigar in his mouth. Although Harper is totally uninterested, Charlie talks about the depressing fact that death cannot be avoided and that what counts nowadays is appearance, not quality.

His watches only seem to remind him that his time is just about up. After lecturing Harper on his lack of courtesy and respect, Charlie complains about the fact that he is not able to keep up with and understand the changes in this world. He declares that the old values of initiative and self-reliance are no longer to be found. Harper, though completely bored, offers Charlie a bit of philosophy, which is flatly rejected. Responding to what he views as impertinence, Charlie declares himself a legend and ejects Harper from the room.

Alone with the porter, he gets the black's confirmation that he was once treated like a hero. The play ends with the two old-timers acknowledging that "Night" has fully arrived.

Tennessee Williams' *The Last of my Solid Gold Watches* (1945) is the study of an old traveling shoe salesman in the American South. He is struggling to come to terms with the fact that the "rush of events" (**49** 26) has left him a lonely misfit who cannot understand and accept the new ways. It is also the study of a man attempting to comprehend and accept the fact that he will soon die.

These two topics suggest that *The Last of my Solid Gold Watches* is both a study of a state of mind and a drama concerned with society. That Charlie is not able to come to terms with the fact that he will soon die is closely connected with his inability to accept and understand – and thus give way to – the times to come. One could say that "the discernible (social) framework serves the individual dilemma."[1] Although Williams might not have had a social play in mind (the way Arthur Miller was preoccupied with the social and political reality that enveloped Willy Loman), a closer look at that "framework" seems justified with regard not only to the particular intentions of this play, but also to Charlie's train of thought.

Talking about "Ole Ben Summers", Charlie begins discussing mortality, the culprit responsible for Ben Summers' death. He becomes depressed and asks, "Who – is going – to prevent it!" (**48** 5) Nodding his head "gravely", he is apparently thinking along lines to which we are not privy. He then continues on an entirely different topic: that of the inferior quality of mod-

1 Marvin Spevack, "Tennessee Williams: The Idea of the Theater," in: *Das amerikanische Drama,* Darmstadt, 1972, p. 257.

ern merchandise. It is not the least bit clear at first what inner logic might explain his saying, "The road is changed. The shoe industry is changed. These times are – revolution!" (**48** 6–7) immediately after discussing the inevitability of death. However, the fact that he uses the same words he used before – "Who is going to prevent it?" (**48** 11) – while carrying on about modern ways is an indication that in his mind there is a connection between the two topics, which would explain the transition from one to the other.

The political and social background of Charlie's unease is made explicit in his long speech on page 49. Explaining to Harper why he dislikes "this new world of yours" (**49** 13), he mentions all the current watchwords of those opposed to President Franklin Delano Roosevelt's New Deal Administration, if only to point out that he does not share these views: a Communist in the White House, Washington in the hands of the Reds, the country's wealth in the hands of Jews (**49** 14–16). The play is set, then, in a period of American history that brought the greatest change ever in the political and economic life of the nation. In his attempt to fight the effects of the Great Depression, Roosevelt created numerous federal agencies (popularly known as "alphabet soup agencies" because of the abbreviations used) and, through the Social Security Act of 1935, set up a system of old-age and unemployment insurance. Conservatives saw in these measures an undermining of those qualities ("initiative – self-reliance" **49** 32) that had made America great. Charlie quite specifically refers to the new government agencies, in particular the AAA (Agricultural Adjustment Act), which aimed at pushing agricultural prices up by reducing the amount of crops produced: "Farmers receivin' payment *not* t' grow wheat an' corn an' *not* t' plant cotton! All of these alphabet letters that's sprung up all about me!" (**49** 22–24)

The changes brought about by the new administration were particularly felt in the agricultural South, for example through the activities of the Tennessee Valley Authority (TVA). It is hardly surprising, then, that Charlie feels that the South's tradition, the "world [he] knew is gone – gone – gone with the wind" (**49** 17–18).

A look at Charlie's environment will show that he associates the political changes with the general picture of deterioration he witnesses about him and, finally, with his own physical decline and impending death. The symbol of the "colored lithograph of blindfolded Hope with her broken lyre" (**43** 12–13) on the wall, the lost grandeur of the hotel room, the "distasteful" literature young Harper devours and the undignified ways in which his old acquaintances have died are all highly suggestive of this.

In the second act of *Period of Adjustment,* Williams states that "dignity too long lost out of the American Dream" has degraded life to a purely materialistic state. And it is exactly this lack of dignity that Charlie cannot accept. After showing the signs of successful salesmanship (fifteen solid-gold Swiss watches, epitomes of everlasting value) to Harper, who is thoroughly uninterested and prefers to be entertained by "the real" *Superman,* Charlie gets excited: "I may have received – the last of my solid gold watches ... But just the same – good manners are still a part of the road's tradition [...] The rudeness – the lack of respect ...!" (**49** 6–25).

This deplorable corruption of values seems to go hand in hand with another change: "STYLE! SMARTNESS! APPEARANCE!" are what count; "The ALL-LEATHER slogan don't sell shoes any more" (**48** 11–13). Charlie complains that the old American values of "initiative – self-reliance – independence of character! The old sterling qualities that distinguished one man from another – the clay from the potters [...] – are [...] Gone with the roses of *yesterday!*" (**49** 32–35).

Charlie's dream has obviously come to an end. The audience/reader will tend to sigh along with the old "war-horse", encouraged by the fact that Harper is set up as an unpleasant contrast to Charlie: "there is no vestige of grandeur in his manner. He is lean and sallow and has a book of colored comics stuffed in his coat pocket" (**44** 35–37).

However, Harper should not be entirely dismissed. He does in fact offer a bit of homely philosophy to Charlie: "In the papers they print people *dead* in one corner and people *born* in the next and usually *one* just about levels *off* with the *other*" (**50** 1–2). Life goes on, and change is one of life's characteristics.

This kind of philosophical approach is just what Charlie needs in order to properly come to terms with his own death and with transitions and value shifts in general.

The play's focus being so clearly on Charlie's personal tragedy, the "new world" does not get equal time, especially as it is represented inadequately by Harper. Harper's function in the play is less to be an ideological counterweight to Charlie than to make Charlie's monologue at all possible. Clearly, the playwright sought to direct the audience's sympathy to the central character. Examining the autobiographical background, one critic has noted that the play represents "a faithful and not unkind sketch of Williams' own father".[2]

---

2 Benjamin Nelson, *Tennessee Williams: The Man and His Work,* New York, 1961, p. 3.

The third character in the play, the old Negro porter, also deserves some attention. At first sight, Charlie's attitude toward the black man may appear to be exclusively characterized by racism (cf. his use of the derogatory terms "darkey" and "nigger" and the way he tosses the second coin to him). A close look will reveal, however, that their relationship is also one of mutual sympathy and respect, even though the underlying basis of their relationship is one where the superiority of the one race over the other is simply assumed by one party and accepted by the other.

Charlie may well see in the black man, "as old as he is" (**43** 24), a mirror image of himself. His comments "You're too old a darkey to tote them big heavy cases" (**43** 30) and "I reckon you'll keep right at it until yuh drop some day" (**44** 2; note that the death theme is here mentioned for the first time) apply to himself as much as they do to the porter. The final scene reverses this pattern of sympathy, with the Black man "gently" (**50** 30) confirming Charlie's visions of the glorious past and "softly, with a wise old smile" (**51** 6) agreeing with Charlie that night has settled. In reply to Charlie's nostalgic "Where have they all gone to?" (**50** 39–40), he explicitly establishes a communion with the white man: "The graveyard is crowded with folks *we* knew" (**51** 1; italics added). The Negro porter and Charlie are presented here as the last remnants of an old order that is quickly passing with what seems to be a final decline of the South. The East with its "Yankee" (or, in Charlie's prejudiced racist view, Jewish) values of industrial production and the fast buck is taking over and hollowing out the old "solid" values.

## First Unit: The Terrible Rush of Events

If this is the first time the students have been confronted with the Southern dialect, it might be necessary to prepare them for the vernacular in the play. A "warning", however, accompanied by one or two examples from the text is quite sufficient.

For example, the first dialogue between Charlie and the porter could be played or read out to the class as an introduction.

As the drama has no innate divisions which would allow for it to be separated into more or less equal sections, we suggest the play should be read completely beforehand, at least in a cursory fashion, or (preferably) listened to on cassette. Since Williams provides such a detailed picture of Charlie's environment and personality, the students will easily be able to imagine the situation. A well-presented dialogue will automatically illustrate the characteristics of Charlie and his manner, which is important for later discussions.

The first assignment of the unit should be dealt with as a talk to the class by a group of interested students or by one individual student. To cope with this task, the students should be given one or several good books on American history, e. g. Samuel Eliot Morison, *The Oxford History of the American People,* New York: Oxford University Press, 1965, pp. 951–970, or John A. Garraty, *American History,* Orlando, Fla.: Harcourt Brace Jovanovich (distributed in Germany by Klett, Klettbuch 51615), 1982, pp. 737–768.

1. *What is the historical background of the play?*
The play obviously does not deal with contemporary America – Charlie's verbal behavior toward the Negro porter would be unimaginable in a contemporary context.

The play was published in 1946, but the period portrayed antedates that year. Charlie's references to the Roosevelt Administration on page 49 and the fact that he laments the passing of the old order with the words "gone with the wind" (**49** 18; Margaret Mitchell's famous novel bearing that title was published in 1936) makes it probable that the play is set some time in the years 1936–1939.

(At this point the prepared talk on the New Deal should be given. Emphasis should especially be put on the opposition to Roosevelt's economic policies.)

2. *What is Charlie's attitude toward the political and economic changes?*
Although he affirms that he does not share the political propaganda of the right (a Communist in the White House, Reds in Washington, country in the hands of Jewish capitalists), he feels that he has witnessed a revolution which has undermined the traditional values of initiative, self-reliance and independence of character.

3. *What other changes is he concerned about?*
All around him, he witnesses signs of deterioration and decay. He sums up his feelings in the remark, "Everything's going downhill around here lately!" (**44** 11–12).

But change for the worse does not stop at hotel rooms and fans that are broken. Charlie's own health is deteriorating, and he shows signs of wear and tear. Add to this what Charlie sees as the decline in quality of contemporary products and the decline of the "human material" he encounters, and we are presented with a very dim picture indeed. "That young fellow,

Mr. Bob Harper" (**44** 24), as Charlie makes clear, is a poor replacement for the old-timers he used to know, just barely enough to prevent him from playing solitaire (**44** 27; cf. **50** 21 where Charlie says that he would rather play solitaire than further associate with Harper).

The most oppressing change that Charlie seems to witness almost daily is the death of his old acquaintances, his colleagues and customers.

4. *When is the death theme first introduced and how is it integrated in the play?*
This theme first appears in Charlie's casual remark to the Negro porter that the latter will probably go on working until he drops dead some day (**44** 2). Throughout the play the theme crops up again and again.

It is interesting to note that Charlie brings up the subject whenever he proudly talks about the products he is selling or about his record as a salesman. No doubt he realizes that, despite his assurance, his firm is no longer "abreast of the times" (**46** 3), that his description of the expected sales success on the following day has more to do with fantasy or reminiscence than with reality (cf. **46** 26–30) and that after forty-six years as a salesman he has come to the end of the road.

In the final part of the play, the subject of death is once again touched upon, this time by the Negro porter as he answers Charlie's lament on the passing of time – "Where have they all gone to?" (**50** 39–40) – with the remark "The graveyard is crowded with folks we knew" (**51** 1).

As the play is so clearly punctuated by this theme, we may assume that this is the change that Charlie fears most, that it is his own impending death he cannot come to terms with. This also becomes clear in his almost violent reaction to Harper's homely philosophy and to his suggestion that Charlie belongs "to the past" (**50** 12).

5. *What is Harper's function in the play?*
Although Charlie attempts to build up Harper as the representative of all the recent changes (cf. his remark "this new world of yours" **49** 13), he remains rather colorless throughout the play. No doubt, his primary function is to serve as a backdrop to Charlie's monologue, barely more than a puppet that will make Charlie's peroration possible.

6. *Does the playwright show sympathy with Charlie and his distress?*
By describing him in words which clearly carry positive connotations ("lavish", "superbly massive", "kingly dignity" **43** 15–16) he marks him as an impressive figure. By referring to his heart problems and loneliness in the hotel, where he is the last of the "ole-timers", Williams evokes the reader's

sympathy for Charlie. His claim that old values such as solidity and quality no longer count is not met by serious protests or alternatives from Harper's side. Harper, the representative of the new ways, is described in very negative terms: he has "never known the 'great days' ...", there "is no vestige of grandeur in his manner", he is "sallow" and has "comics stuffed in his coat pocket" (**44** 35–37).

7. *One critic has pointed out that in this play Williams has drawn a sketch of his own father. How could one characterize the playwright's attitude toward the protagonist in this play?*

Williams portrays a man who is eager for life and who cannot come to terms with the passing of time and his own mortality. Although he certainly seems to be critical of his character in this respect, the salesman's portrait is executed with sympathy and with understanding for his tragedy.

## Second Unit: The Role of the Porter / Symbolism

1. *How, at first sight, would you characterize Charlie's attitude toward the Negro porter?*
(See above p. 88)

2. *Describe the relationship between Charlie and the porter.*
Their relationship is also one of mutual sympathy and respect. Williams seems to be more interested in showing a common humanity existing between the two men than in exploring a racially determined relationship.

(Note: The students will be interested in the following anecdote from Williams' own life which would indicate that the playwright would not use the word "nigger" lightly: When he was a child he is supposed to have hurt his nanny's feelings by calling her a "nigger". The black nurse left the Williams' home before the boy had a chance to apologize, resulting in his carrying a psychological scar from the incident for a great many years.[3])

3. *At what two points does the porter appear on the scene? Is there any difference in Charlie's behavior in the two scenes?*
The scenes in which the Negro porter appears serve to frame the piece, and by this token gain a certain importance. There is indeed a marked difference between the two scenes. Although he "puffs and rumbles" (**43** 17) when he first enters the hotel, Charlie still displays his usual "kingly dignity

3 Nancy Tischler, *Tennessee Williams,* Austin, 1969, p. 14.

of bearing" (**43** 16). His behavior toward the porter is here in accordance with his status: it is he who pities the old man and offers consolation as well as a tip.

In the final scene, Charlie is a broken man, and it is now up to the black man to console him. It is now the porter who has taken over the role in which Harper, in Charlie's understanding of it, had so miserably failed. Charlie can again evoke the glorious past and he has a willing and understanding audience (as it were, the porter is now "tipping" Charlie). But at the same time the Negro porter can make the same point Harper had tried to make, only more gently, more solemnly, more softly: "The graveyard is filled with folks we knew" (**51** 1). It is because he and the white man share a common humanity that the black porter is so much more successful in bringing Charlie to an understanding of his own situation.

4. *Comment on the symbolism in the play.*
The symbolism is heavy, particularly at the end of the play where Charlie throws up the blinds to show that it is night. We were, however, prepared for this symbolic ending by the stage direction given at the beginning of the play (**44** 29). (Note: the students might be interested to hear what Williams himself said about the use of symbols: "Symbols are nothing but the natural speech of drama."[4] "... a symbol in a play has only one legitimate purpose, which is to say a thing more directly and simply [...] than it could be said in words."[5])

## For Further Study and Discussion

1. It is a widespread belief, especially among older people, that "everything's going downhill." Discuss this attitude.

2. Write an essay in which you describe the value shifts between your own world and your parents' world as you see them.

3. Read Arthur Miller's *Death of a Salesman* and compare Willy Loman with Charlie, and Miller's treatment of the subject of change (values, dreams, preferences, frustration) with Williams'. Compare the authors' social and political commitments.

---

4 Quoted by Klaus Lubbers, "Tennessee Williams," in: Martin Christadler, ed., *Amerikanische Literatur der Gegenwart,* Stuttgart, 1973, p. 433.

5 Quoted by Frederick Lumley, *New Trends in Twentieth Century Drama: A Survey since Ibsen and Shaw,* London, 1972, p. 168.

4. Try to see the film version of *A Streetcar Named Desire* by Elia Kazan, USA 1951, with Vivien Leigh as Blanche DuBois and Marlon Brando as Stanley Kowalski; see how their acting supports the clash of different worlds, values and personality types.

Compare *A Streetcar Named Desire* with *The Last of My Solid Gold Watches*.

5. Does Williams' view of the American South correspond to your notions? Discuss whether the play could just as well take place in a different part of the U.S.A. or even in Germany.

Edward Albee

# The Zoo Story

The Players:

PETER:

*A man in his early forties, neither fat nor gaunt, neither handsome nor homely. He wears tweeds, smokes a pipe, carries horn-rimmed glasses. Although he is moving into middle age, his dress and his manner would suggest a man younger.*

JERRY:

*A man in his late thirties, not poorly dressed, but carelessly. What was once a trim and lightly muscled body has begun to go to fat; and while he is no longer handsome, it is evident that he once was. His fall from physical grace should not suggest debauchery; he has, to come closest to it, a great weariness.*

The Scene:

*It is Central Park; a Sunday afternoon in summer; the present. There are two park benches, one toward either side of the stage; they both face the audience. Behind them: foliage, trees, sky. At the beginning, Peter is seated on one of the benches.*

Stage Directions:

*As the curtain rises, Peter is seated on the bench stage-right. He is reading a book. He stops reading, cleans his glasses, goes back to reading. Jerry enters.*

JERRY I've been to the zoo. *(Peter doesn't notice)* I said, I've been to the zoo. MISTER, I'VE BEEN TO THE ZOO!

PETER Hm? ... What? ... I'm sorry, were you talking to me?

JERRY I went to the zoo, and then I walked until I came here. Have I been walking north?

PETER *(puzzled)* North? Why ... I ... I think so. Let me see.

JERRY *(pointing past the audience)* Is that Fifth Avenue?

PETER Why yes; yes, it is.

JERRY And what is that cross street there; that one, to the right?

PETER That? Oh, that's Seventy-fourth Street.

JERRY And the zoo is around Sixty-fifth Street; so, I've been walking north.

PETER *(anxious to get back to his reading)* Yes; it would seem so.

JERRY Good old north.

PETER *(lightly, by reflex)* Ha, ha.

JERRY *(after a slight pause)* But not due north.

PETER I ... well, no, not due north; but, we ... call it north. It's northerly.

JERRY *(watches as Peter, anxious to dismiss him, prepares his pipe)* Well, boy; *you're* not going to get lung cancer, are you?

PETER *(looks up, a little annoyed, then smiles)* No, sir. Not from this.

JERRY No, sir. What you'll probably get is cancer of the mouth, and then you'll have to wear one of those things Freud wore after they took one whole side of his jaw away. What do they call those things?

PETER *(uncomfortable)* A prosthesis?

JERRY The very thing! A prosthesis. You're an educated man, aren't you? Are you a doctor?

PETER Oh, no; no. I read about it somewhere; *Time* magazine, I think. *(He turns to his book.)*

JERRY Well, *Time* magazine isn't for blockheads.

PETER No, I suppose not.

JERRY *(after a pause)* Boy, I'm glad that's Fifth Avenue there.

PETER *(vaguely)* Yes.

JERRY I don't like the west side of the park much.

PETER Oh? *(then, slightly wary, but interested)* Why?

JERRY *(offhand)* I don't know.

PETER Oh. *(He returns to his book.)*

JERRY *(He stands for a few seconds, looking at Peter, who finally looks up again, puzzled.)* Do you mind if we talk?

PETER *(obviously minding)* Why ... no, no.

JERRY Yes you do; you do.

PETER *(Puts his book down, his pipe out and away, smiling.)* No, really; I don't mind.

JERRY Yes you do.

PETER *(finally decided)* No; I don't mind at all, really.

JERRY It's ... it's a nice day.

PETER *(stares unnecessarily at the sky)* Yes. Yes, it is; lovely.

JERRY I've been to the zoo.

PETER Yes, I think you said so ... didn't you?

JERRY You'll read about it in the papers tomorrow, if you don't see it on your TV tonight. You have TV, haven't you?

PETER Why yes, we have two; one for the children.

JERRY You're married!

PETER *(with pleased emphasis)* Why, certainly.

JERRY It isn't a law, for God's sake.

PETER No ... no, of course not.

JERRY And you have a wife.

PETER *(bewildered by the seeming lack of communication)* Yes!

JERRY And you have children.

PETER Yes; two.

JERRY Boys?

PETER No, girls ... both girls.

JERRY But you wanted boys.

PETER Well ... naturally, every man wants a son, but ...

JERRY *(lightly mocking)* But that's the way the cookie crumbles?

PETER *(annoyed)* I wasn't going to say that.

JERRY And you're not going to have any more kids, are you?

PETER *(a bit distantly)* No. No more. *(then back, and irksome)* Why did you say that? How would you know about that?

JERRY The way you cross your legs, perhaps; something in the voice. Or maybe I'm just guessing. Is it your wife?

PETER *(furious)* That's none of your business! *(a silence)* Do you understand? *(Jerry nods. Peter is quiet now.)* Well, you're right. We'll have no more children.

JERRY *(softly)* That *is* the way the cookie crumbles.

PETER *(forgiving)* Yes ... I guess so.

JERRY Well, now; what else?

PETER What were you saying about the zoo ... that I'd read about it, or see ...?

JERRY I'll tell you about it, soon. Do you mind if I ask you questions?

PETER Oh, not really.

JERRY I'll tell you why I do it; I don't talk to many people – except to say like: give me a beer, or where's the john, or what time does the feature go on, or keep your hands to yourself, buddy. You know – things like that.

PETER I must say I don't ...

JERRY But every once in a while I like to talk to somebody, really *talk;* like to get to know somebody, know all about him.

PETER *(lightly laughing, still a little uncomfortable)* And am I the guinea pig for today?

JERRY On a sun-drenched Sunday afternoon like this? Who better than a nice married man with two daughters and ... uh ... a dog? *(Peter shakes his head.)* No? Two dogs. *(Peter shakes his head again.)* Hm. No dogs? *(Peter shakes his head, sadly.)* Oh, that's a shame. But you look like an animal man. CATS? *(Peter nods his head, ruefully.)* Cats! But, that can't be your idea. No, sir. Your wife and daughters? *(Peter nods his head.)* Is there anything else I should know?

PETER *(He has to clear his throat.)* There are ... there are two parakeets. One ... uh ... one for each of my daughters.

JERRY Birds.

PETER My daughters keep them in a cage in their bedroom.

JERRY Do they carry disease? The birds.

PETER I don't believe so.

JERRY That's too bad. If they did you could set them loose in the house and the cats could eat them and die, maybe. *(Peter looks blank for a moment, then laughs.)* And what else? What do you do to support your enormous household?

PETER I ... uh ... I have an executive position with a ... a small publishing house. We ... uh ... we publish textbooks.

JERRY That sounds nice; very nice. What do you make?

PETER *(still cheerful)* Now look here!

JERRY Oh, come on.

PETER Well, I make around eighteen thousand a year, but I don't carry more than forty dollars at any one time ... in case you're a ... a holdup man ... ha, ha, ha.

JERRY *(ignoring the above)* Where do you live? *(Peter is reluctant.)* Oh, look; I'm not going to rob you, and I'm not going to kidnap your parakeets, your cats, or your daughters.

PETER *(too loud)* I live between Lexington and Third Avenue, on Seventy-fourth Street.

JERRY That wasn't so hard, was it?

PETER I didn't mean to seem ... ah ... it's that you don't really carry on a conversation; you just ask questions, and I'm ... I'm normally ... uh ... reticent. Why do you just stand there?

JERRY I'll start walking around in a little while, and eventually I'll sit down. *(recalling)* Wait until you see the expression on his face.

PETER What? Whose face? Look here; is this something about the zoo?

JERRY *(distantly)* The what?

PETER The zoo; the zoo. Something about the zoo.

JERRY The zoo?

PETER You've mentioned it several times.

JERRY *(still distant, but returning abruptly)* The zoo? Oh, yes; the zoo. I was there before I came here. I told you that. Say, what's the dividing line between upper-middle-middle-class and lower-upper-middle-class?

PETER My dear fellow, I ...

JERRY Don't my dear fellow me.

PETER *(unhappily)* Was I patronizing? I believe I was; I'm sorry. But, you see, your question about the classes bewildered me.

JERRY And when you're bewildered you become patronizing?

PETER I ... I don't express myself too well, sometimes. *(He attempts a joke on himself.)* I'm in publishing, not writing.

JERRY *(amused, but not at the humor)* So be it. The truth *is I* was being patronizing.

PETER Oh, now; you needn't say that.

*(It is at this point that Jerry may begin to move about the stage with slowly increasing determination and authority, but pacing himself, so that the long speech about the dog comes at the high point of the arc.)*

JERRY All right. Who are your favorite writers? Baudelaire and J. P. Marquand?

PETER *(Wary)* Well, I like a great many writers; I have a considerable ... catholicity of taste, if I may say so. Those two men are fine, each in his way. *(warming up)* Baudelaire, of course ... uh ... is by far the finer of the two, but Marquand has a place ... in our ... uh ... national ...

JERRY Skip it.

PETER I ... sorry.

JERRY Do you know what I did before I went to the zoo today? I walked all the way up Fifth Avenue from Washington Square; all the way.

PETER Oh; you live in the Village! *(This seems to enlighten Peter.)*

JERRY No, I don't. I took the subway down to the Village so I could walk all the way up Fifth Avenue to the zoo. It's one of those things a person has to do; sometimes a person has to go a very long distance out of his way to come back a short distance correctly.

PETER *(almost pouting)* Oh, I thought you lived in the Village.

JERRY What were you trying to do? Make sense out of things? Bring order? The old pigeonhole bit? Well, that's easy; I'll tell you. I live in a four-story brownstone rooming-house on the upper West Side between Columbus Avenue and Central Park West. I live on the top floor; rear; west. It's a laughably small room, and one of my walls is made of beaverboard; this beaverboard separates my room from another laughably small room, so I assume that the two rooms were once one room, a small room, but not necessarily laughable. The room beyond my beaverboard wall is occupied by a colored queen who always keeps his door open; well, not always, but *always* when he's plucking his eyebrows, which he does with

Buddhist concentration. This colored queen has rotten teeth, which is rare, and he has a Japanese kimono, which is also pretty rare; and he wears this kimono to and from the john in the hall, which is pretty frequent. I mean, he goes to the john a lot. He never bothers me, and he never brings anyone up to his room. All he does is pluck his eyebrows, wear his kimono and go to the john. Now, the two front rooms on my floor are a little larger, I guess; but they're pretty small, too. There's a Puerto Rican family in one of them, a husband, a wife, and some kids; I don't know how many. These people entertain a lot. And in the other front room, there's somebody living there, but I don't know who it is. I've never seen who it is. Never. Never ever.

PETER *(embarrassed)* Why ... why do you live there?

JERRY *(from a distance again)* I don't know.

PETER It doesn't sound like a very nice place ... where you live.

JERRY Well, no; it isn't an apartment in the East Seventies. But, then again, I don't have one wife, two daughters, two cats and two parakeets. What I do have, I have toilet articles, a few clothes, a hot plate that I'm not supposed to have, a can opener, one that works with a key, you know; a knife, two forks, and two spoons, one small, one large; three plates, a cup, a saucer, a drinking glass, two picture frames, both empty, eight or nine books, a pack of pornographic playing cards, regular deck, an old Western Union typewriter that prints nothing but capital letters, and a small strongbox without a lock which has in it ... what? Rocks! Some rocks ... sea-rounded rocks I picked up on the beach when I was a kid. Under which ... weighed down ... are some letters ... please letters ... please why don't you do this, and please when will you do that letters. And when letters, too. When will you write? When will you come? When? These letters are from more recent years.

PETER *(stares glumly at his shoes, then)* About those two empty picture frames ...?

JERRY I don't see why they need any explanation at all. Isn't it clear? I don't have pictures of anyone to put in them.

PETER Your parents ... perhaps ... a girl friend ...

JERRY You're a very sweet man, and you're possessed of a truly enviable innocence. But good old Mom and good old Pop are dead ... you know? ... I'm broken up about it, too ... I mean really. BUT. That particular vaudeville act is playing the cloud circuit now, so I don't see how I can look at them, all neat and framed. Besides, or, rather, to be pointed about it, good old Mom walked out on good old Pop when I was ten and a half years old; she embarked on an adulterous turn of our southern states

... a journey of a year's duration ... and her most constant companion ... among others, among many others ... was a Mr. Barleycorn. At least, that's what good old Pop told me after he went down ... came back ... brought her body north. We'd received the news between Christmas and New Year's, you see, that good old Mom had parted with the ghost in some dump in Alabama. And, without the ghost ... she was less welcome. I mean, what was she? A stiff ... a northern stiff. At any rate, good old Pop celebrated the New Year for an even two weeks and then slapped into the front of a somewhat moving city omnibus, which sort of cleaned things out family-wise. Well no; then there was Mom's sister, who was given neither to sin nor the consolations of the bottle. I moved in on her, and my memory of her is slight excepting I remember still that she did all things dourly: sleeping, eating, working, praying. She dropped dead on the stairs to her apartment, my apartment then, too, on the afternoon of my high school graduation. A terribly middle-European joke, if you ask me.

PETER Oh, my; oh, my.

JERRY Oh, your what? But that was a long time ago, and I have no feeling about any of it that I care to admit to myself. Perhaps you can see, though, why good old Mom and good old Pop are frameless. What's your name? Your first name?

PETER I'm Peter.

JERRY I'd forgotten to ask you. I'm Jerry.

PETER *(with a slight, nervous laugh)* Hello, Jerry.

JERRY *(nods his hello)* And let's see now; what's the point of having a girl's picture, especially in two frames? I have two picture frames, you remember. I never see the pretty little ladies more than once, and most of them wouldn't be caught in the same room with a camera. It's odd, and I wonder if it's sad.

PETER The girls?

JERRY No. I wonder if it's sad that I never see the little ladies more than once. I've never been able to have sex with, or, how is it put? ... make love to anybody more than once. Once; that's it. ... Oh, wait; for a week and a half, when I was fifteen ... and I hang my head in shame that puberty was late ... I was a h-o-m-o-s-e-x-u-a-l. I mean, I was queer ... *(very fast)* ... queer, queer, queer ... with bells ringing, banners snapping in the wind. And for those eleven days, I met at least twice a day with the park superindendent's son ... a Greek boy, whose birthday was the same as mine, except that he was a year older. I think I was very much in love ... maybe just with sex. But that was the jazz of a very special hotel, wasn't it? And now; oh, do I love the little ladies; really, I love them. For about an hour.

PETER Well, it seems perfectly simple to me. ...

JERRY *(angry)* Look! Are you going to tell me to get married and have parakeets?

PETER *(angry himself)* Forget the parakeets! And stay single if you want to. It's no business of mine. I didn't start this conversation in the ...

JERRY All right, all right. I'm sorry. All right? You're not angry?

PETER *(laughing)* No, I'm not angry.

JERRY *(relieved)* Good. *(Now back to his previous tone.)* Interesting that you asked me about the picture frames. I would have thought that you would have asked me about the pornographic playing cards.

PETER *(with a knowing smile)* Oh, I've seen those cards.

JERRY That's not the point. *(laughs)* I suppose when you were a kid you and your pals passed them around, or you had a pack of your own.

PETER Well, I guess a lot of us did.

JERRY And you threw them away just before you got married.

PETER Oh, now; look here. I didn't *need* anything like that when I got older.

JERRY No?

PETER *(embarrassed)* I'd rather not talk about these things.

JERRY So? Don't. Besides, I wasn't trying to plumb your post-adolescent sexual life and hard times; what I wanted to get at is the value difference between pornographic playing cards when you're a kid, and pornographic playing cards when you're older. It's that when you're a kid you use the cards as a substitute for a real experience, and when you're older you use real experience as a substitute for the fantasy. But I imagine you'd rather hear about what happened at the zoo.

PETER *(enthusiastic)* Oh, yes; the zoo. *(then, awkward)* That is ... if you. ...

JERRY Let me tell you about why I went ... well, let me tell you some things. I've told you about the fourth floor of the roominghouse where I live. I think the rooms are better as you go down, floor by floor. I guess they are; I don't know. I don't know any of the people on the third and second floors. Oh, wait! I do know that there's a lady living on the third floor, in the front. I know because she cries all the time. Whenever I go out or come back in, whenever I pass her door, I always hear her crying, muffled, but ... very determined. Very determined indeed. But the one I'm getting to, and all about the dog, is the landlady. I don't like to use words that are too harsh in describing people. I don't like to. But the landlady is a fat, ugly, mean, stupid, unwashed, misanthropic, cheap, drunken bag of garbage. And you may have noticed that I very seldom use profanity, so I can't describe her as well as I might.

PETER You describe her ... vividly.

JERRY Well, thanks. Anyway, she has a dog, and I will tell you about the dog, and she and her dog are the gatekeepers of my dwelling. The woman is bad enough; she leans around in the entrance hall, spying to see that I don't bring in things or people, and when she's had her mid-afternoon pint of lemon-flavored gin she always stops me in the hall, and grabs ahold of my coat or my arm, and she presses her disgusting body up against me to keep me in a corner so she can talk to me. The smell of her body and her breath ... you can't imagine it ... and somewhere, somewhere in the back of that pea-sized brain of hers, an organ developed just enough to let her eat, drink, and emit, she has some foul parody of sexual desire. And I, Peter, I am the object of her sweaty lust.

PETER That's disgusting. That's ... horrible.

JERRY But I have found a way to keep her off. When she talks to me, when she presses herself to my body and mumbles about her room and how I should come there, I merely say: but, Love; wasn't yesterday enough for you, and the day before? Then she puzzles, she makes slits of her tiny eyes, she sways a little, and then, Peter ... and it is at this moment that I think I might be doing some good in that tormented house ... a simple-minded smile begins to form on her unthinkable face, and she giggles and groans as she thinks about yesterday and the day before; as she believes and relives what never happened. Then, she motions to that black monster of a dog she has, and she goes back to her room. And I am safe until our next meeting.

PETER It's so ... unthinkable. I find it hard to believe that people such as that really *are*.

JERRY *(lightly mocking)* It's for reading about, isn't it?

PETER *(seriously)* Yes.

JERRY And fact is better left to fiction. You're right, Peter. Well, what I have been meaning to tell you about is the dog; I shall, now.

PETER *(nervously)* Oh yes; the dog.

JERRY Don't go. You're not thinking of going, are you?

PETER Well ... no, I don't think so.

JERRY *(as if to a child)* Because after I tell you about the dog, do you know what then? Then ... then I'll tell you about what happened at the zoo.

PETER *(laughing faintly)* You're ... you're full of stories, aren't you?

JERRY You don't *have* to listen. Nobody is holding you here; remember that. Keep that in your mind.

PETER *(irritably)* I know that.

JERRY You do? Good. *(The following long speech, it seems to me, should be done with a great deal of action, to achieve a hypnotic effect on Peter, and on the audience, too. Some specific actions have been suggested, but the director and the actor playing Jerry might best work it out for themselves.)* ALL RIGHT. *(As if reading from a huge billboard.)* THE STORY OF JERRY AND THE DOG! *(Natural again.)* What I am going to tell you has something to do with how sometimes it's necessary to go a long distance out of the way in order to come back a short distance correctly; or, maybe I only think that it has something to do with that. But, it's why I went to the zoo today, and why I walked north ... northerly, rather ... until I came here. All right. The dog, I think I told you, is a black monster of a beast: an oversized head, tiny, tiny ears, and eyes ... bloodshot, infected, maybe; and a body you can see the ribs through the skin. The dog is black, all black; all black except for the bloodshot eyes, and ... yes ... and an open sore on its ... *right* forepaw; that is red, too. And, oh yes; the poor monster, and I do believe it's an old dog ... it's certainly a misused one ... almost always has an erection ... of sorts. That's red, too. And ... what else? ... oh, yes; there's a gray-yellow-white color, too, when he bares his fangs. Like this: Grrrrrrr! Which is what he did when he saw me for the first time ... the day I moved in. I worried about that animal the very first minute I met him. Now, animals don't take to me like Saint Francis had birds hanging off him all the time. What I mean is: animals are indifferent to me ... like people *(He smiles slightly.)* ... most of the time. But this dog wasn't indifferent. From the very beginning he'd snarl and then go for me, to get one of my legs. Not like he was rabid, you know; he was sort of a stumbly dog, but he wasn't half-assed, either. It was a good, stumbly run; but I always got away. He got a piece of my trouser leg, look, you can see right here, where it's mended; he got that the second day I lived there; but I kicked free and got upstairs fast, so that was that. *(puzzles)* I still don't know to this day how the other roomers manage it, but you know what I *think:* I think it had only to do with me. Cozy. So. Anyway, this went on for over a week, whenever I came in; but never when I went out. That's funny. Or, it *was* funny. I could pack up and live in the street for all the dog cared. Well, I thought about it up in my room one day, one of the times after I'd bolted upstairs, and I made up my mind. I decided: First, I'll kill the dog with kindness, and if that doesn't work ... I'll just kill him. *(Peter winces)*

Don't react, Peter; just listen. So, the next day I went out and bought a bag of hamburgers, medium rare, no catsup, no onion; and on the way home I threw away all the rolls and kept just the meat. *(Action for the following, perhaps.)* When I got back to the roominghouse the dog was waiting for me. I half opened the door that led into the entrance hall, and there he was; waiting for me. It figured. I went in, very cautiously, and I had the hamburgers, you remember; I opened the bag, and I set the meat down about twelve feet from where the dog was snarling at me. Like so! He snarled; stopped snarling; sniffed; moved slowly; then faster; then faster toward the meat. Well, when he got to it he stopped, and he looked at me. I smiled; but tentatively, you understand. He turned his face back to the hamburgers, smelled, sniffed some more, and then ... RRRAAAAGGGGGHHHH, like that ... he tore into them. It was as if he had never eaten anything in his life before, except like garbage. Which might very well have been the truth. I don't think the landlady ever eats anything but garbage. But. He ate all the hamburgers, almost all at once, making sounds in his throat like a woman. *Then,* when he'd finished the meat, the hamburger, and tried to eat the paper, too, he sat down and smiled. I think he smiled; I know cats do. It was a very gratifying few moments. Then, BAM, he snarled and made for me again. He didn't get me this time, either. So, I got upstairs, and I lay down on my bed and started to think about the dog again. To be truthful, I was offended, and I was damn mad, too. It was six perfectly good hamburgers with not enough pork in them to make it disgusting. I was offended. But, after a while, I decided to try it for a few more days. If you think about it, this dog had what amounted to an antipathy toward me; really. And, I wondered if I mightn't overcome this antipathy. So, I tried it for five more days, but it was always the same: snarl, sniff; move; faster; stare; gobble; RAAGGGHHH; smile; snarl; BAM. Well, now; by this time Columbus Avenue was strewn with hamburger rolls and I was less offended than disgusted. So, I decided to kill the dog. *(Peter raises a hand in protest.)* Oh, don't be so alarmed, Peter; I didn't succeed. The day I tried to kill the dog I bought only one hamburger and what I thought was a murderous portion of rat poison. When I bought the hamburger I asked the man not to bother with the roll, all I wanted was the meat. I expected some reaction from him, like: we don't sell no hamburgers without rolls; or, wha' d'ya wanna do, eat it out'a ya han's? But no; he smiled benignly, wrapped up the hamburger in waxed paper, and said: A bite for ya pussycat? I wanted to say: No, not really; it's part of a plan to poison a dog I know. But, you can't say "a dog I know" without sounding funny; so I said, a little too loud, I'm afraid, and too formally: YES, A BITE FOR MY PUSSY-CAT. People looked up. It always happens when I try to simplify things; people look up. But that's neither hither nor thither. So. On my way back to the roominghouse, I kneaded the hamburger and the rat poison together between my hands, at that point feeling as much sadness as disgust. I opened the door to the entrance hall, and there the monster was, waiting to take the offering and then jump me. Poor bastard; he never learned that the moment he took to smile before he went for me gave me time enough to get out of range. BUT, there he was; malevolence with an erection, waiting. I put the poison patty down, moved toward the stairs and watched. The poor animal gobbled the food down as usual, smiled, which made me almost sick, and then, BAM. But, I sprinted up the stairs, as usual, and the dog didn't get me, as usual. AND IT CAME TO PASS THAT THE BEAST WAS DEATHLY ILL. I knew this because he no longer attended me, and because the landlady sobered up. She stopped me in the hall the same evening of the attempted murder and confided the information that God had struck her puppy-dog a surely fatal blow. She had forgotten her bewildered lust, and her eyes were wide open for the first time. They looked like the dog's eyes. She sniveled and implored me to pray for the animal. I wanted to say to her: Madam, I have myself to pray for, the colored queen, the Puerto Rican family, the person in the front room whom I've never seen, the woman who cries deliberately behind her closed door, and the rest of the people in all roominghouses, everywhere; besides, Madam, I don't understand how to pray. But ... to simplify things ... I told her I would pray. She looked up. She said that I was a liar, and that I probably wanted the dog to die. I told her, and there was so much truth here, that I didn't want the dog to die. I didn't, and not just because I'd poisoned him. I'm afraid that I must tell you I wanted the dog to live so that I could see what our new relationship might come to. *(Peter indicates his increasing displeasure and slowly growing antagonism.)* Please understand, Peter; that sort of thing is important. You must believe me; it *is* important. We have to know the effect of our actions. *(Another deep sigh.)* Well, anyway; the dog recovered. I have no idea why, unless he was a descendant of the puppy that guarded the gates of hell or some such resort. I'm not up on my mythology. (*He pronounces the word myth-o-*logy.) Are you? *(Peter sets to thinking, but Jerry goes on.)* At any rate, you've missed the eight-thousand-dollar question, Peter; at any rate, the dog recovered his health and the landlady recovered her thirst, in no way altered by the bow-wow's deliverance. When I came home from a movie that was playing on Forty-second Street, a movie I'd seen, or one that was very much like one or several I'd seen, after the landlady told me puppykins was better, I was so hoping for the dog to be waiting for me. I was ... well, how would you put it ... enticed? ... fascinated? ... no, I don't think so ... heart-shatteringly anxious, that's it; I was heart-shatteringly anxious to confront my friend again. *(Peter reacts scoffingly.)* Yes, Peter; friend. That's the only word for it. I was heart-shatteringly et cetera to confront my doggy friend again. I came in the door and advanced, unafraid, to the center of the entrance hall. The beast was there ... looking at me. And, you know, he looked better for his scrape with the nevermind. I stopped; I looked at him; he looked at me. I think ... I think we stayed a long time that way ... still, stone-statue ... just looking at one another. I looked more into his face than he looked into mine. I mean, I can concentrate longer at looking into a dog's face than a dog can concentrate at looking into mine, or into anybody else's face, for that matter. But during that twenty seconds or two hours that we looked into each other's face, we made contact. Now, here is what I had wanted to happen: I loved the dog now, and I wanted him to love me. I had tried to love, and I had tried to kill, and both had been unsuccessful by themselves. I hoped ... and I don't really know why I expected the dog to understand anything, much less my motivations ... I hoped that the dog would understand. *(Peter seems to be hypnotized.)* It's just ... it's just that ... *(Jerry is abnormally tense, now.)* ... it's just that if you can't deal with people, you have to make a start somewhere. WITH ANIMALS! *(Much faster now, and like a conspirator.)* Don't you see? A person has to have some way of dealing with SOMETHING. If not with people ... if not with people ... SOMETHING. With a bed, with a cockroach, with a mirror ... no, that's too hard, that's one of the last steps. With a cockroach, with a ... with a ... with a carpet, a roll of toilet paper ... no, not that, either ... that's a mirror, too; always check bleeding. You see how hard it is to find things? With a street corner, and too many lights, all colors reflecting on the oily-wet streets ... with a wisp of smoke, a wisp ... of smoke ... with ... with pornographic playing cards, with a strongbox ... WITHOUT A LOCK ... with love, with vomiting, with crying, with fury because the pretty little ladies aren't pretty little ladies, with making money with your body which is an act of love and I could prove it, with howling because you're alive; with God. How about that? WITH GOD WHO IS A COLORED QUEEN WHO WEARS A KIMONO AND PLUCKS HIS EYEBROWS, WHO IS A WOMAN WHO CRIES WITH DETERMINATION BEHIND HER CLOSED DOOR ...with

God who, I'm told, turned his back on the whole thing some time ago ... with ... some day, with people. *(Jerry sighs the next word heavily.)* People. With an idea; a concept. And where better, where ever better in this humiliating excuse for a jail, where better to communicate one single, simple-minded idea than in an entrance hall? Where? It would be A START! Where better to make a beginning ... to understand and just possibly be understood ... a beginning of an understanding, than with ... *(Here Jerry seems to fall into almost grotesque fatigue.)* ... than with A DOG. Just that; a dog. *(Here there is a silence that might be prolonged for a moment or so; then Jerry wearily finishes his story.)* A dog. It seemed like a perfectly sensible idea. Man is a dog's best friend, remember. So: the dog and I looked at each other. I longer than the dog. And what I saw then has been the same ever since. Whenever the dog and I see each other we both stop where we are. We regard each other with a mixture of sadness and suspicion, and then we feign indifference. We walk past each other safely; we have an understanding. It's very sad, but you'll have to admit that it is an understanding. We had made many attempts at contact, and we had failed. The dog has returned to garbage, and I to solitary but free passage. I have not returned. I mean to say, I have *gained* solitary free passage, if that much further loss can be said to be gain. I have learned that neither kindness nor cruelty by themselves, independent of each other, creates any effect beyond themselves; and I have learned that the two combined, together, at the same time, are the teaching emotion. And what is gained is loss. And what has been the result: the dog and I have attained a compromise; more of a bargain, really. We neither love nor hurt because we do not try to reach each other. And, *was* trying to feed the dog an act of love? And, perhaps, was the dog's attempt to bite me *not* an act of love? If we can so misunderstand, well then, why have we invented the word love in the first place? *(There is silence. Jerry moves to Peter's bench and sits down beside him. This is the first time Jerry has sat down during the play.)* The Story of Jerry and the Dog: the end. *(Peter is silent.)* Well, Peter? *(Jerry is suddenly cheerful.)* Well, Peter? Do you think I could sell that story to the *Reader's Digest* and make a couple of hundred bucks for *The Most Unforgettable Character I've Ever Met?* Huh? *(Jerry is animated, but Peter is disturbed.)* Oh, come on now, Peter; tell me what you think.

PETER *(numb)* I ... I don't understand what ... I don't think I ... *(Now, almost tearfully.)* Why did you tell me all of this?

JERRY Why not?

PETER I DON'T UNDERSTAND!

JERRY *(furious, but whispering)* That's a lie.

PETER No. No, it's not.

JERRY *(quietly)* I tried to explain it to you as I went along. I went slowly; it all has to do with ...

PETER I DONT WANT TO HEAR ANY MORE. I don't understand you, or your landlady, or her dog. ...

JERRY *Her* dog! I thought it was my ... No. No, you're right. It *is* her dog. *(Looks at Peter intently, shaking his head.)* I don't know what I was thinking about; of course you don't understand. *(In a monotone, wearily.)* I don't live in your block; I'm not married to two parakeets, or whatever your setup is. I am a *permanent transient,* and my home is the sickening roominghouses on the West Side of New York City, which is the greatest city in the world. Amen.

PETER I'm ... I'm sorry; I didn't mean to ...

JERRY Forget it. I suppose you don't quite know what to make of me, eh?

PETER *(a joke)* We get all kinds in publishing. *(Chuckles)*

JERRY You're a funny man. *(He forces a laugh.)* You know that? You're a very ... a richly comic person.

PETER *(modestly, but amused)* Oh, now, not really. *(Still chuckling)*

JERRY Peter, do I annoy you, or confuse you?

PETER *(lightly)* Well, I must confess that this wasn't the kind of afternoon I'd anticipated.

JERRY You mean, I'm not the gentleman you were expecting.

PETER I wasn't expecting anybody.

JERRY No, I don't imagine you were. But I'm here, and I'm not leaving.

PETER *(consulting his watch)* Well, you may not be, but I must be getting home soon.

JERRY Oh, come on; stay a while longer.

PETER I really should get home; you see ...

JERRY *(tickles Peter's ribs with his fingers)* Oh, come on.

PETER *(He is very ticklish; as Jerry continues to tickle him his voice becomes falsetto.)* No, I ... OHHHHH! Don't do that. Stop, stop. Ohhh, no, no.

JERRY Oh, come on.

PETER *(as Jerry tickles)* Oh, hee, hee, hee. I must go. I ... hee, hee, hee. After all, stop, stop, hee, hee, hee, after all, the parakeets will be getting dinner ready soon. Hee, hee. And the cats are setting the table. Stop, stop, and, and ... *(Peter is beside himself now)* ... and we're having ... hee, hee ... uh ... ho, ho, ho. *(Jerry stops tickling Peter, but the combination of the tickling and his own mad whimsy has Peter laughing almost hysterically. As his laughter continues, then subsides, Jerry watches him, with a curious fixed smile.)*

JERRY Peter?

PETER Oh, ha, ha, ha, ha, ha. What? What?

JERRY Listen, now.

PETER Oh, ho, ho. What ... what is it, Jerry? Oh, my.

JERRY *(mysteriously)* Peter, do you want to know what happened at the zoo?

PETER Ah, ha, ha. The what? Oh, yes; the zoo. Oh, ho, ho. Well, I had my own zoo there for a moment with ... hee, hee, the parakeets getting dinner ready, and the ... ha, ha, whatever it was, the ...

JERRY *(calmly)* Yes, that was very funny, Peter. I wouldn't have expected it. But do you want to hear about what happened at the zoo, or not?

PETER Yes. Yes, by all means; tell me what happened at the zoo. Oh, my. I don't know what happened to me.

JERRY Now I'll let you in on what happened at the zoo; but first, I should tell you why I went to the zoo. I went to the zoo to find out more about the way people exist with animals, and the way animals exist with each other, and with people too. It probably wasn't a fair test, what with everyone separated by bars from everyone else, the animals for the most part from each other, and always the people from the animals. But, if it's a zoo, that's the way it is. *(He pokes Peter on the arm.)* Move over.

PETER *(friendly)* I'm sorry, haven't you enough room? *(He shifts a little.)*

JERRY *(smiling slightly)* Well, all the animals are there, and all the people are there, and it's Sunday and all the children are there. *(He pokes Peter again.)* Move over.

PETER *(patiently, still friendly)* All right. *(He moves some more, and Jerry has all the room he might need.)*

JERRY And it's a hot day, so all the stench is there, too, and all the balloon sellers, and all the ice cream sellers, and all the seals are barking, and all the birds are screaming. *(Pokes Peter harder.)* Move over!

PETER *(beginning to be annoyed)* Look here, you have more than enough room! *(But he moves more, and is now fairly cramped at one end of the bench.)*

JERRY And I am there, and it's feeding time at the lions' house, and the lion keeper comes into the lion cage, one of the lion cages, to feed one of the lions. *(Punches Peter on the arm, hard.)* MOVE OVER!

PETER *(very annoyed)* I can't move over any more, and stop hitting me. What's the matter with you?

JERRY Do you want to hear the story? *(Punches Peter's arm again.)*

PETER *(flabbergasted)* I'm not so sure! I certainly don't want to be punched in the arm.

JERRY *(punches Peter's arm again)* Like that?

PETER Stop it! What's the matter with you?

JERRY I'm crazy, you bastard.

PETER That isn't funny.

JERRY Listen to me, Peter. I want this bench. You go sit on the bench over there, and if you're good I'll tell you the rest of the story.

PETER *(flustered)* But ... whatever for? What *is* the matter with you? Besides, I see no reason why I should give up this bench. I sit on this bench almost every Sunday afternoon, in good weather. It's secluded here; there's never anyone sitting here, so I have it all to myself.

JERRY *(softly)* Get off this bench, Peter; I want it.

PETER *(almost whining)* No.

JERRY I said I want this bench, and I'm going to have it. Now get over there.

PETER People can't have everything they want. You should know that; it's a rule; people can have some of the things they want, but they can't have everything.

JERRY *(laughs)* Imbecile! You're slow-witted!

PETER Stop that!

JERRY You're a vegetable! Go lie down on the ground.

PETER *(intense)* Now *you* listen to me. I've put up with you all afternoon.

JERRY Not really.

PETER LONG ENOUGH. I've put up with you long enough. I've listened to you because you seemed ... well, because I thought you wanted to talk to somebody.

JERRY You put things well; economically, and, yet ... oh, what is the word I want to put justice to your ... JESUS, you make me sick ... get off here and give me my bench.

PETER MY BENCH!

JERRY *(pushes Peter almost, but not quite, off the bench)* Get out of my sight.

PETER *(regaining his position)* God da ... mn you. That's enough! I've had enough of you. I will not give up this bench; you can't have it, and that's that. Now, go away. *(Jerry snorts but does not move.)* Go away, I said. *(Jerry does not move.)* Get away from here. If you don't move on ... you're a bum ... that's what you are. ... If you don't move on, I'll get a policeman here and make you go. *(Jerry laughs, stays.)* I warn you, I'll call a policeman.

JERRY *(softly)* You won't find a policeman around here; they're all over on the west side of the park chasing fairies down from trees or out of the bushes. That's all they do. That's their function. So scream your head off; it won't do you any good.

PETER POLICE! I warn you, I'll have you arrested. POLICE! *(Pause)* I said POLICE! *(Pause)* I feel ridiculous.

JERRY You look ridiculous: a grown man screaming for the police on a bright Sunday afternoon in the park with nobody harming you. If a policeman *did* fill his quota and come sludging over this way he'd probably take you in as a nut.

PETER *(with disgust and impotence)* Great God, I just came here to read, and now you want me to give up the bench. You're mad.

JERRY Hey, I got news for you, as they say. I'm on your precious bench, and you're never going to have it for yourself again.

PETER *(furious)* Look, you; get off my bench. I don't care if it makes any sense or not. I want this bench to myself; I want you OFF IT!

JERRY *(mocking)* Aw ... look who's mad.

PETER GET OUT!

JERRY No.

PETER I WARN YOU!

JERRY Do you know how ridiculous you look *now?*

PETER *(His fury and self-consciousness have possessed him.)* It doesn't matter. *(He is almost crying.)* GET AWAY FROM MY BENCH!

JERRY Why? You have everything in the world you want; you've told me about your home, and your family, and *your own* little zoo. You have everything, and now you want this bench. Are these the things men fight for? Tell me, Peter, is this bench, this iron and this wood, is this your honor? Is this the thing in the world you'd fight for? Can you think of anything more absurd?

PETER Absurd? Look, I'm not going to talk to you about honor, or even try to explain it to you. Besides, it isn't a question of honor; but even if it were, you wouldn't understand.

JERRY *(contemptuously)* You don't even know what you're saying, do you? This is probably the first time in your life you've had anything more trying to face than changing your cat's toilet box. Stupid! Don't you have any idea, not even the slightest what other people *need?*

PETER Oh, boy, listen to you; well, you don't need this bench. That's for sure.

JERRY Yes; yes, I do.

PETER *(quivering)* I've come here for years; I have hours of great pleasure, great satisfaction, right here. And that's important to a man. I'm a responsible person, and I'm a GROWNUP. This is my bench, and you have no right to take it away from me.

JERRY Fight for it, then. Defend yourself; defend your bench.

PETER You've *pushed* me to it. Get up and fight.

JERRY Like a man?

PETER *(still angry)* Yes, like a man, if you insist on mocking me even further.

JERRY I'll have to give you credit for one thing; you *are* a vegetable, and a slightly nearsighted one, I think ...

PETER THAT'S ENOUGH. ...

JERRY ... but, you know, as they say on TV all the time – you know – and I mean this, Peter, you have a certain dignity; it surprises me. ...

PETER STOP!

JERRY *(rises lazily)* Very well, Peter, we'll battle for the bench, but we're not evenly matched. *(He takes out and clicks open an ugly-looking knife.)*

PETER *(suddenly awakening to the reality of the situation)* You *are* mad! You're stark raving mad! YOU'RE GOING TO KILL ME! *(But before Peter has time to think what to do, Jerry tosses the knife at Peter's feet.)*

JERRY There you go. Pick it up. You have the knife and we'll be more evenly matched.

PETER *(horrified)* No!

JERRY *(rushes over to Peter, grabs him by the collar; Peter rises; their faces almost touch)* Now you pick up that knife and you fight with me. You fight for your self-respect; you fight for that goddamned bench.

PETER *(struggling)* No! Let ... let go of me! He ... Help!

JERRY *(slaps Peter on each "fight")* You fight, you miserable bastard; fight for that bench; fight for your parakeets; fight for your cats, fight for your two daughters; fight for your wife; fight for your manhood, you pathetic little vegetable. *(Spits in Peter's face.)* You couldn't even get your wife with a male child.

PETER *(breaks away, enraged)* It's a matter of genetics, not manhood, you ... you monster. *(He darts down, picks up the knife and backs off a little; he is breathing heavily.)* I'll give you one last chance; get out of here and leave me alone! *(He holds the knife with a firm arm, but far in front of him, not to attack, but to defend.)*

JERRY *(sighs heavily)* So be it! *(With a rush he charges Peter and impales himself on the knife. Tableau: For just a moment, complete silence, Jerry impaled on the knife at the end of Peter's still firm arm. Then Peter screams, pulls away, leaving the knife in Jerry. Jerry is motionless, on point. Then he, too, screams, and it must be the sound of an infuriated and fatally wounded animal. With the knife in him, he stumbles back to the bench that Peter had vacated. He crumbles there; sitting, facing Peter, his eyes wide in agony, his mouth open.)*

PETER *(whispering)* Oh my God, oh my God, oh my God. ... *(He repeats these words many times, very rapidly.)*

JERRY *(Jerry is dying; but now his expression seems to change. His features relax, and while his voice varies, sometimes wrenched with pain, for the most part he seems removed from his dying. He smiles.)* Thank you, Peter. I mean that, now; thank you very much. *(Peter's mouth drops open. He cannot move; he is transfixed.)* Oh, Peter, I was so afraid I'd drive you away. *(He laughs as best he can.)* You don't know how afraid I was you'd go away and leave me. And now I'll tell you what happened at the zoo. I think ... I think this is what happened at the zoo ... I think. I think that while I was at the zoo I decided that I would walk north ... northerly, rather ... until I found you ... or somebody ... and I decided that I would talk to you ... I would tell you things ... and things that I would tell you would ... Well, here we are. You see? Here we *are*. But ... I don't know ... could I have planned all this? No ... no, I couldn't have. But I think I did. And now I've told you what you wanted to know, haven't I? And now you know all about what happened at the zoo. And now you know what you'll see in your TV, and the face I told you about ... you remember ... the face I told you about ... my face, the face you see right now. Peter ... Peter? ... Peter ... thank you. I came unto you *(He laughs, so faintly.)* and you have comforted me. Dear Peter.

PETER *(almost fainting)* Oh my God!

JERRY You'd better go now. Somebody might come by, and you don't want to be here when anyone comes.

PETER *(does not move, but begins to weep)* Oh my God, oh my God.

JERRY *(most faintly, now; he is very near death)* You won't be coming back here any more, Peter; you've been dispossessed. You've lost your bench, but you've defended your honor. And Peter, I'll tell you something now; you're not really a vegetable; it's all right, you're an animal. You're an animal, too. But you'd better hurry now, Peter. Hurry, you'd better go ... see? *(Jerry takes a handkerchief and with great effort and pain wipes the knife handle clean of fingerprints.)* Hurry away, Peter. *(Peter begins to stagger away.)* Wait ... wait, Peter. Take your book ... book. Right here ... beside me ... on your bench ... my bench, rather. Come ... take your book. *(Peter starts for the book, but retreats.)* Hurry ... Peter. *(Peter rushes to the bench, grabs the book, retreats.)* Very good, Peter ...

very good. Now ... hurry away. *(Peter hesitates for a moment, then flees, stage left.)* Hurry away. ... *(His eyes are closed now.)* Hurry away, your parakeets are making the dinner ... the cats ... are setting the table ...

PETER *(off stage)* *(A pitiful howl.)* OH MY GOD!

JERRY *(His eyes still closed, he shakes his head and speaks; a combination of scornful mimicry and supplication.)* Oh ... my ... God. *(He is dead.)*

*Curtain*

## Biographical Notes

*Edward Albee, one of America's most original playwrights, was adopted in 1928 when he was two weeks old by the wealthy owner of a chain of vaudeville theaters. His childhood seems to have been that of "The Poor Little Rich Boy". When he was twenty, he began a somewhat bohemian decade in Manhattan with the purpose of becoming a writer.*

*His New York years represent a difficult period in his life. It was at the height of despair over the course his life had taken that, in 1957, he sat down on the eve of his thirtieth birthday to type out "The Zoo Story" on a wobbly kitchen table.*

*With his "Zoo Story", Albee commanded attention; with "Who's Afraid of Virginia Woolf?" (first produced in 1962), he became famous.*

*Albee took the theater world by storm and was heralded as the American representative of the "Theater of the Absurd". Albee embraces this group's fundamental assertion that the human condition is essentially meaningless. "We do not have to live unless we wish to; the greatest sin in living is doing it badly ... stupidly, or as if you were not alive", he once declared. "All serious art", he has said, "is an attempt to modify and change people's perception of themselves, to bring them into larger contact with the fact of being alive." As for his method, he believes in provocation: "If the theater must bring us only what we can immediately apprehend or comfortably relate to, let us stop going to the theater entirely ..." He once said that people should come away from a performance "having suffered an experience of some sort ..."*

*His fame rests on "The Zoo Story" and "Who's Afraid of Virginia Woolf?" but Albee has written many other plays. "The Sandbox" (1959), "The American Dream" (1960), "Tiny Alice" (1965), "A Delicate Balance" (1966), "Box and Quotations from Chairman Mao Tse-Tung" (1969) and "All Over" (1971) are among the most important ones.*

**Annotations**

**54** 3 **gaunt** [gɔ:nt] lean, skinny – 4 **homely** not handsome; ugly – **horn-rimmed glasses** spectacles with frame made of material resembling (animal) horn – 9 **trim** in shape, fit – 10 **his fall from physical grace ...** the fact that he is no longer handsome – 11 **debauchery** [dɪ'bɔ:tʃərɪ] indulgence in sensual pleasures – 12 **weariness** tiredness, fatigue – 14 **Central Park** a large park in the center of Manhattan Island – 16 **foliage** ['fəʊlɪɪdʒ] leaves

**55** 4 **due** *adv.* directly, exactly – 6 **to dismiss** to send away – 11 **jaw** *Kiefer* – 12 **prosthesis** [prɒs'θi:sɪs] – 17 **blockhead** slow and stupid person – 22 **wary** ['weərɪ] careful, cautious – 23 **offhand** spontaneous, without thought

**56** 5 **bewildered** [bɪ'wɪldəd] puzzled, confused – 12 **that's the way the cookie crumbles** *(coll.)* there's nothing one can do – 15 **irksome** ['ɜ:ksəm] upset; annoyed – 19 **furious** extremely angry – 30 **john** *(sl.)* toilet – **feature** full-length film in a cinema program – 31 **buddy** *(sl.)* fellow – 35 **guinea pig** ['gɪnɪ] *Meerschweinchen; hier: Versuchskaninchen* – 37 **sun-drenched** soaked with sunshine

**57** 1 **ruefully** ['ru:fʊlɪ] pitifully, sadly, expressing regret – 4 **parakeet** *(A.E.)* budgerigar – 15 **textbook** book for use in school or university – 16 **what do you make?** *(informal)* how much do you earn? – 19 **eighteen thousand** (a considerable amount at the time the play was written) – 20 **holdup** robbery – 30 **reticent** ['retɪsənt] not saying much – 31 **eventually** finally, in the end – 32 **to recall** to bring back to the mind, to remember

**58** 3 **to patronize** ['pætrənaɪz] to treat s.o. as if he were an inferior person – 12 **to pace** to walk at a carefully determined step – 13 **arc** part of a circle – 17 **catholicity** [––'–––] a wide range, a great number of things – 20 **skip it** *(coll.)* forget it – 24 **the Village** Greenwich Village, area of lower Manhattan where many artists live – **to enlighten** to make s.o. see clearly – 29 **to pout** [paʊt] *schmollen* – 31 **to pigeonhole** to put into (too) neat categories – **the old ... bit** *(coll.)* (a way of saying that s.th. is a common phenomenon) – 32 **brownstone** a typical building material of NYC houses – **rooming-house** *(A.E.)* a house where apartments and rooms are for rent – 34 **beaverboard** *Preßplatte* – 38 **queen** *(sl.)* a male homosexual who likes to appear as a female – 39 **to pluck** to pull out, usually one-by-one

**59** 1 **Buddhist concentration** total concentration – **rotten** decayed; having gone bad – 9 **to entertain** [ˌentə'teɪn] to have guests, visitors – 12 **(to be/feel) embarrassed** [ɪm'bærəst] to be ashamed, uneasy – 17 **hot plate** electric heater used to cook food – 21 **a deck** (of cards) a pack of playing cards – 23 **strongbox** *Geldkassette* – 29 **glum** gloomy, sad – 34 **enviable** ['envɪəbl] *beneidenswert* – 36 **to be broken up about s.th.** *(coll.)* to be extremely sad about s.th. – 37 **vaudeville** ['vɔ:dəvɪl] *(French)* a comic theatrical piece – **that particular ... is playing the cloud circuit** ['sɜ:kɪt] my parents are dead and in heaven (rather disrespectful) – 39 **to walk out on** to leave – 40 **to embark on** to engage in any enterprise – **adulterous turn** [ə'dʌltərəs] a tour/trip involving sexual relationships with men other than her husband

**60** 2 **Mr. Barleycorn** = John Barleycorn *(coll.),* whiskey (made from barley); an allusion to Jerry's mother being an alcoholic – 5 **to part with the ghost** to die – 6 **dump** *(sl.)* cheap, unattractive hotel or apartment house – **a stiff** *(sl.)* a dead body – 8 **for an even two weeks** for all of two weeks – 10 **family-wise** *(coll.)* in terms of the family – 11 **to be given to s.th.** to have as a habit – **consolation** comfort – 13 **dour** ['dʊə] severe; stern – 17 **oh, my** *(short for:)* oh, my goodness – 35 **queer** *(sl.)* homosexual – 38 **superintendent** *(A.E.)* person in charge of the upkeep of a building or, here, a park

**61** 15 **pal** *(coll.)* friend – 22 **to plumb** [plʌm] to get to the root of – **post-adolescent** [ˌædə'lesnt] when you're about to become an adult – 38 **muffled** indistinct – 40 **harsh** severe, cruel

**62** 1 **misanthropic** [ˌmɪsn'θrɒpɪk] hating or distrusting human society – 3 **profanity** [prə'fænɪtɪ] bad, vulgar language – 4 **vivid** clear, distinct – 6 **dwelling** ['dwelɪŋ] the place where s.o. lives – 14 **to emit** to give or send out – **foul parody** disgusting imitation – 21 **to sway** to move unsteadily, first to one side, then to the other – 22 **tormented** [tɔ:'mentɪd] suffering – 24 **to groan** *stöhnen* – 40 **faint** weak; indistinct

**63** 3 **irritably** showing annoyance, anger – 8 **billboard** large advertisement sign, e.g. at the roadside – 16 **bloodshot** *blutunterlaufen* – 18 **paw** animal's foot – 22 **bares his fangs** shows his teeth – 28 **to snarl** to show the teeth and growl – **to go for s.o.** to attack – 29 **rabid** ['ræbɪd] affected with rabies *(Tollwut)*; mad – **stumbly** not walking with sureness – 30 **half-assed** *(sl.)* clumsy, imperfect – 35 **cozy** (usually said of a room) warm and comfortable – 38 **to bolt** [bəʊlt] to run away quickly – 40 **to wince** [wɪns] to make a facial gesture indicating mental pain or distress

**64** 2 **medium rare** not cooked completely – **catsup** ketchup – 6 **it figured** *(coll.)* that was to be expected – 11 **tentative** ['– – –] hesitant, careful – 19 **gratifying** satisfying, giving pleasure – 28 **to gobble** to eat fast, greedily, and noisily – 30 **to strew** to throw all over, to scatter – 37 **benign** [bɪ'naɪn] kind and gentle

**65** 3 **that's neither hither nor thither** *(coll.)* that's neither here nor there; that's irrelevant – 4 **to knead** [ni:d] to mix and shape with one's hands – 7 **poor bastard** (suggests pity mixed with hostility) – 9 **out of range** beyond reach – 10 **malevolence** [–'– – –] evil will – **patty** a round, flattened out piece of ground meat – 14 **it came to pass** highly formal, old-fashioned phrase (biblical language) – 16 **to sober up** ['səʊbə] to become serious; not be drunk any more – 17 **to confide s.th. to s.b.** [kən'faɪd] *anvertrauen* – 18 **fatal** ['feɪtl] deadly – 20 **to snivel** ['snɪvl] to complain in a miserable, whining way – **to implore** [ɪm'plɔ:] *anflehen* – 23 **deliberately** [dɪ'lɪbrətlɪ] (done) on purpose – 35 **resort** *(here iron.)* a popular place of entertainment or recreation (cf. a seaside resort) – **to be up on s.th.** *(coll.)* to be well-informed about s.th. – 40 **bow-wow** (baby talk) dog – **deliverance** rescue

**66** 4 **enticed** [ɪn'taɪst] tempted – 5 **heart-shatteringly** to an extreme degree – 6 **to scoff** to mock – 10 **scrape with the nevermind** *here:* encounter with death – 27 **cockroach** ['kɒkrəʊtʃ] *Kakerlake* – 32 **wisp** thin, twisted piece of s.th. – 34 **to vomit** *sich übergeben* – 35 **fury** anger

**67** 4 **to humiliate** [hjʊ'mɪlɪeɪt] to cause s.o. to feel ashamed – **jail** prison – 8 **fatigue** [fə'ti:g] condition of being very tired – 15 **to feign** [feɪn] to pretend – 19 **solitary** lonely; without companions – 25 **to attain** [ə'teɪn] to reach, arrive at – 34 **buck** *(sl.)* dollar – 35 **animated** ['– – – –] lively – 37 **numb** [nʌm] without ability to feel or move

**68** 8 **intently** [ɪn'tentlɪ] eagerly; earnestly – 11 **setup** ['setʌp] *(coll.)* arrangement, constellation – **transient** ['trænzɪənt] *(as noun, A.E.)* person who is not settled, who comes and goes – 16 **to chuckle** to laugh with mouth closed – 20 **to annoy** [ə'nɔɪ] to cause inconvenience, to irritate – 22 **to anticipate** [–'– – –] to expect – 26 **to consult** to ask for advice, to look for information – 30 **to tickle** *kitzeln* – 32 **falsetto** [fɔ:l'setəʊ] unnaturally high-pitched voice in men – 38 **to be beside o.s.** to be out of control – 40 **whimsy** odd humor

**69** 1 **to subside** to become less – 22 **to poke** [pəʊk] to push with a stick, one's finger etc. – 23 **to shift** to move – 29 **stench** extremely unpleasant smell – 30 **seal** [si:l] *Seehund* – 37 **to punch** to hit hard with the fist

**70** 1 **to flabbergast** ['flæbəgɑ:st] to astonish – 9 **to fluster** to make nervous or confused – 11 **secluded** [sɪ'klu:dɪd] hidden, isolated – 14 **to whine** to complain in long-drawn sounds (like a dog, a siren etc.) – 20 **imbecile** ['ɪmbɪsi:l] idiot – **slow-witted** mentally slow – 23 **to put up with s.o. or s.th.** to tolerate s.o. or s.th. – 36 **to snort** to force the air with violence through the nose; to laugh loudly – 38 **bum** person leading an unsteady life

**71** 2 **fairy** *here: (sl.)* homosexual – 9 **quota** ['kwəʊtə] *here:* number of arrests a policeman is supposed to make – **to sludge** *etwa: vorbeischlappen* – 10 **nut** *(sl.)* person who is crazy – 11 **impotence** lack of strength or power – 33 **contemptuous** [kən'temptʃʊəs] completely disrespectful; disdaining – 34 **trying** difficult, challenging – 40 **to quiver** ['kwɪvə] to shake with excitement

**72** 9 **to give s.o. credit for s.th.** *here:* to assure s.o. of s.th. – 16 **to be evenly matched** to do s.th. under the same conditions, with the same equipment –

18 **stark raving mad** absolutely crazy – 19 **to toss** to throw with a quick, light motion – 29 **pathetic** [pə'θetɪk] pitiful – 30 **to get** = beget; to father, make pregnant – 32 **enraged** extremely angry – 33 **to dart** to move rapidly – 37 **to impale** [ɪm'peɪl] to pierce with s.th. sharp – 38 **tableau** scene

**73** 3 **to vacate** ['veɪkeɪt] to quit, to leave – **to crumble** *here:* to collapse – 4 **agony** extreme pain – 7 **his features relax** his face becomes less tense – 8 **wrenched** [rentʃt] violently twisted – 11 **transfixed** [–'–] held fixed or motionless – 31 **to dispossess** [ˌdɪspə'zes] to put out of possession – 37 **to stagger** to walk unsteadily, as from weakness or drunkenness – 39 **to retreat** to move back

**74** 6 **scornful mimicry** disrespectful imitation – **supplication** [ˌsʌplɪ'keɪʃn] humble prayer, asking for mercy, help etc.

# Interpretation and Teaching Notes

## Content and Analysis

Peter is seated on a bench in Central Park one Sunday afternoon. He is a smartly-dressed middle-aged man, reading a book. Jerry, younger and carelessly dressed, enters and announces he has been to the zoo. He prevents Peter, who is smoking a pipe, from dismissing him by telling him he will get cancer of the mouth. Peter, a reader of *Time* magazine, consents to talk with Jerry, although he obviously minds.

Jerry manages to extract quite a lot from Peter, in spite of the latter's reticence. He learns that he is married, has two children and two TVs, cats and two parakeets. He has an executive position with a textbook publisher, earns a highly respectable income and has a highly respectable address (he lives on the upper East Side). Invited to talk about his favorite authors, Peter holds forth in a sterile manner on Baudelaire and J. P. Marquand, only to be cut short by Jerry.

Jerry lives on the upper West Side in a miserable rooming house, the description of which discomforts Peter. A list of Jerry's belongings includes two empty picture frames, rocks kept from childhood days, and more recent "please letters." Jerry glibly describes how he lost both his parents when he was ten, and goes on to reveal that he cannot make love to any woman more than once. He did have, however, an intense, though short-lived, homosexual relationship when he was fifteen. Jerry embarrasses Peter, who eagerly encourages him to talk about the zoo instead. But Jerry has to explain more about his rooming house before he can explain what happened at the zoo. Describing the landlady as repugnant and revealing how he avoids her sexual advances by feeding her fantasies, Jerry once again causes Peter, who can hardly believe such people exist, deep discomfort.

Then Jerry begins what he calls "The Story of Jerry and the Dog." Jerry tells about the landlady's dog who used to meet Jerry with a certain antipathy whenever Jerry entered the house. After failing to buy the dog's friendship with hamburgers, he tried to poison it. He was relieved, though, when the dog did not die, hoping to see if their relationship might not come to something. He reveals to Peter that he had hoped to learn how to relate to people by beginning modestly – starting with objects and animals, and then progressing to human beings. Although the end result was indifference on the dog's part and not the kind of "relationship" Jerry had hoped for,

Jerry did learn that only through a combination of kindness *and* cruelty could he have any effect on someone or something else.

Peter is deeply upset by the story. He declares he does not want to hear any more and tries to compensate his discomfort with a joke. Abandoning his verbal approach to Peter, Jerry begins to tickle him.

Jerry explains that he went to the zoo to find out more about the relationship between people and animals. What he found is that animals are neatly separated from each other and the people. Then he begins a final assault upon Peter, hitting him and finally claiming the bench for himself. Peter resists the takeover, making a complete fool of himself in the process. Jerry responds with outright contempt, declaring that Peter is a mere vegetable. A battle for the bench ensues, in the course of which Jerry throws himself onto a knife he had tossed to Peter to even out the contest.

Dying, he says he could not have planned what happened, but thinks he did. He thanks Peter, who is horrified. Jerry declares that Peter has been dispossessed of his bench for good, but concedes that he is not really a vegetable, but an animal. Wiping off Peter's fingerprints before he flees, Jerry shows both disdain and love for Peter before finally dying.

Edward Albee's *The Zoo Story* (1958) depicts the need to reach out and establish contact with other human beings. At the same time the pursuit of the "good life" interferes with this aim and thereby interferes with humanity. Albee shows two characters who are polar opposites. There is a wide spectrum of responses to this play, ranging from seeing Jerry as somewhat perverse to proclaiming him a saint.[1] The fact that Albee himself admitted in an interview, "There are some things in it I don't really understand,"[2] makes it frustratingly difficult to attempt a coherent interpretation.

At first glance, the representative upper-middle-class figure Peter seems to be a man who has obviously "made it," and who is fairly secure in the materialistic things in life. A closer look at the stage directions reveals a bit more: "Although he is moving into middle age, his dress and manner would suggest a man younger" (**54** 5–6). This seems to translate into: "Peter is the kind of person who cannot accept that he is growing older, and who therefore tries to cover up his mortality by cultivating a younger look; he believes in appearances." The case against our pipe-smoking executive builds up when, "anxious to dismiss" Jerry (**55** 6), he tries to make his lack of interest

1 See W. M. Force, "The *What* Story? Or, Who's at the Zoo?" *Costerus* 2, 1972, pp. 71–82, for a good review of the various positions.

2 *New York Times,* February 15, 1960, p. 23.

clear by occupying himself with his pipe, even though Jerry has done very little at this point to justify such dismissal.

The over-polite behavior he reveals a little later results from a way of life which stresses, above all, the cultivation of a surface where one is always supposed to "be nice". Peter does indeed mind Jerry's offer to talk, but he lacks the courage to say so!

When we learn that "why, certainly" (**56** 1) he is married and that he has a "naturally-every-man-wants-a-son" attitude towards children, we are quite ready to place Peter into the pigeonhole we reserve for all people who, through the pursuit of the good life and the resulting materialism and conformity, lose all individual integrity whatsoever.

Gradually, however, after our initial dismissal of Peter, we feel some sympathy for him, namely at the point where Jerry imposes himself rather outrageously upon him. The problem is that Jerry is so strange. The play seems to condemn the Peters of the world who, by becoming wrapped up in materialism and superficial concerns, are no longer able to respond to other human beings. Jerry, by contrast, appears to be a "great communicator".

Jerry is highly bizarre, having apparently had a traumatic childhood. He is something of a deviate, suffering from personal problems arising from his unique circumstances. The list he gives of his belongings provides some clues as to his problems. The two "picture frames, both empty" (**59** 20) apparently represent the fact that the loss of both parents at a young age deeply disturbed him and still does. It becomes clear, then, after what is a rather black-and-white opening, that the play is as much about Jerry's peculiar personal problems as it is an exposé of Peter and his having "sold out". That Jerry is the non-conformist he is seems to prevent us from embracing him as the desirable alternative to Peter. But Jerry, at least, is unique, where Peter is colorless.

It is strange that Albee presents one character with all his peculiar traits and the other as if he had no uniqueness, no particular past. But the point is not that Peter has no particular past, giving rise to particular and perhaps peculiar traits, but that he has allowed his uniqueness to be blotted out by the demands of his lifestyle. Jerry qualifies for our interest by recognizing the need to reach out beyond his own limited self in order to embrace humanity. He is genuinely aware of his existential isolation and the need to make an effort to transcend it.

Jerry's particular program for learning how to reach beyond his limited self – involving overtures to inanimate objects, animals and, finally, other people – may seem ridiculous and even absurd, but it is actually a fascinating and, if you will, a respectable undertaking. The program involves recognizing one's imprisonment in the ego and devising a science of sorts which will teach one how to break through the bars of that prison.

With this explanation as a background, Jerry's selecting Peter makes more sense. It is one last desperate effort at reaching out and establishing contact, in spite of what he learned at the zoo, where everyone is separated from everyone else by bars. That the encounter did not satisfy Jerry's needs is, however, not Peter's fault alone: Jerry insists on treating Peter with as much contempt as concern. The discovery that one does not necessarily approach others with an undiluted outpouring of empathy, but with a mixture of empathy and disgust, or cruelty and kindness, seems to derive from his experience with the dog.

Along with Jerry's sexuality (more precisely homosexuality, which is hinted at throughout the text), this helps to understand the ambivalence in his attitude towards Peter. As a specimen of humanity, Peter is of the highest interest to Jerry in his attempt to come into contact with other human beings. But as a specimen of the kind of individual who gives up his true humanity, Peter is revolting. He prides himself in being "a responsible person, and [...] a GROWNUP" (**72** 2), yet behaves utterly childishly when Jerry demands the bench. That Jerry is "wrong" in insisting on having the bench for himself alone is not really up for discussion. What Albee wants to show is that Peter insists on his right to the bench to the point of absurdity.

What Albee is getting at depends largely upon how one interprets Jerry's making Peter the agent of his death. The spectrum of responses to this central part of the play can be reduced to the following three positions: The first is that Jerry, being at the end of his rope, "wants out" and selects Peter as the agent of his yearned-for death. At the same time he attains a certain revenge on Peter as a symbol of that which has made his reaching-out more difficult.

The second position, presented by Richard Kostelanetz, has it that the play describes "at base ... a failed homosexual pass," pointing to various references throughout the play which, taken together, indicate an overwhelming homosexual preoccupation on the part of the protagonist. This line of argument leads to the following interpretation of the play's ending: "Culminating the surrogate seduction, Jerry impales himself upon [the knife's] blade [an erect phallus] with rhythms suggestive of an orgasm."[3]

The third approach, presented by Rose Zimbardo, is generous, arguing that Jerry is a saint – indeed a "modernized Messiah." Zimbardo goes on to

---

3 Richard Kostelanetz, "Edward Albee," in: *On Contemporary Literature,* ed. R. Kostelanetz, New York 1964, pp. 225, 227.

say that "Jerry dies for Peter ... to save Peter's soul from death by spiritual starvation."[4]

Let us try to sort things out somewhat.

As for seeing Jerry's self-orchestrated murder in purely selfish terms, it should be clear enough that, although he is certainly caught up in his purely personal problem, he is nonetheless led beyond the purely personal sphere in seeking to understand and deal with his isolation. And if the play ends with his "scornful mimicry" of Peter, that final expression of cruelty contains at the same time an expression of kindness, of something the opposite of hostility, as the word "supplication" connotes.

As for seeing *The Zoo Story* as being in essence nothing more than "a failed homosexual pass," it should be mentioned that there is absolutely nothing in the play which would allow a director to have Jerry impale himself on the blade "with rhythms suggestive of an orgasm"! This ridiculous interpretation aside, though, there are indeed hints of homosexuality throughout the play, and it is instructive to think about this approach. Let us assume that Jerry's interactions with Peter are sexually motivated, at least partially. Why would we not be able, in such a case, to see the desire for sex as *one* legitimate response to existential anxiety, that is, loneliness? Jerry certainly has his sights set on something more than mere sexuality when he talks about the need to reach out beyond the self and explains his graduated program. Sexual desire does not necessarily contradict what Jerry is striving for. It could very well exist as an undercurrent to his notion of communication.

As for seeing Jerry as a savior, it should first be mentioned that Zimbardo's article does not take into account the "cruelty" aspect of Jerry's behavior. Although Albee uses the word "supplication", which has an ecclesiastical meaning (a humble prayer to God for mercy, aid, or some special blessing), it does not necessarily imply that Jerry has a traditional Christian world view. The phrase "Oh my God" – a standard one used by Christians and non-Christians alike – is Peter's. Jerry is merely imitating it. When Jerry refers to God, "who ... turned his back on the whole thing some time ago" (**67** 1), he seems to be revealing his acceptance of standard twentieth century agnosticism or atheism. Indeed, he suggests that for him, God is located within the realm of humanity, not above it ("You have to make a start somewhere ... WITH GOD WHO IS A COLORED QUEEN

4 Rose Zimbardo, "Symbolism and Naturalism in Edward Albee's *The Zoo Story,*" *Twentieth Century Literature* 8, 1962, p. 16

WHO WEARS A KIMONO AND PLUCKS HIS EYEBROWS; WHO IS A WOMAN WHO CRIES ..." **66** 37–40).

It is possible to see *The Zoo Story* as being a highly moral play, without its necessarily having to be religious. Could not Jerry set up his own death for accutely personal reasons, while at the same time making a personal sacrifice in order to bring about Peter's salvation by shocking him out of his complacency?

Albee has attempted to settle the controversy about the ending by saying that it is "neither nihilistic nor pessimistic ... My hero is not a beatnik and he is not insane. He is over-sane. Though he dies, he passes on an awareness of life to the other character in the play; the play, therefore, is obviously not a denial of life."[5]

Remembering that Jerry is at one and the same time kind and cruel towards Peter, there is no reason to deny him the higher motives ascribed to him in forcing Peter to participate in his death. We certainly would not want to argue, however, that Peter suddenly "sees the light" and reforms his ways. Indeed, one wonders if an individual such as Peter would not want to repress what happened and continue with his previous way of life. But Albee seems to suggest that Peter's moral annihilation is a certain salvation. The question "what happens after the curtain falls?" is absolutely appropriate for *The Zoo Story* (unlike many other plays), but *not* because we have to decide what happens to Peter. Rather, through our debate about "Peter's future," we are forced to think about the issues raised in this play, thereby having our own attitudes and lives affected. It may be that Albee is less interested in what Peter's future life might be like, in how the experience might have affected him, than in shocking his audience into the recognition that they are themselves like Peter, that they are unable to communicate with each other – and that they had better do something about this.

There is much of the absurd in *The Zoo Story,* but not of the metaphysical or ontological sort, as it is to be found in many other modern plays. In *The Zoo Story,* absurdity is not an *a priori* condition: We *make* life absurd by choosing a way which blinds us to what our real concerns ought to be. Jerry – especially in his overtures to the dog – seems at first absolutely ludicrous. But Jerry, for all his deviateness, is not nearly as absurd as Peter, who, with "impotence", tries to defend his so-called honor.

However, while emerging as the play's hero, Jerry is not without his limitations. Thus, in attempting a final assessment of *The Zoo Story,* one

5 Quoted in Michael Rutenberg, *Edward Albee: Playwright in Protest,* New York 1969, p. 37.

comes to the conclusion that neither the one nor the other character in the play "stands for" an approach to life that would find our approval. Rather the playwright has presented to us what the human zoo of our everyday lives looks like.

## First Unit: The Plot

The students should be familiar with the entire play before interpreting it. As *The Zoo Story* is the longest and the most difficult play in this sequence, it is necessary to divide it into digestible sections which should be read in class or listened to on cassette rather than at home. We suggest a combination of aural presentation (preferably on cassette) and private reading phases to prepare a passage or to study it further.

Depending on how advanced the students are, several divisions are possible, e.g.:

a) beginning of play – **56** 36
**56** 37 – **60** 24
**60** 25 – **63** 3
**63** 4 – **68** 6
**68** 7 – **72** 36
**72** 37 – end of play

b) beginning of play – **63** 3
**63** 4 – **68** 6
**68** 7 – end of play

c) beginning of play – **63** 3
**63** 4 – end of play.

The tape should be stopped after these sections and the plot should be summarized orally. After this, the first homework could be given before analyzing the drama.

**Homework:**
Write a brief but comprehensive plot summary of *The Zoo Story*. Concern yourself only with what happens in the play, not its meaning or significance. (Only summarize the basic elements of the play's plot.)

## Second Unit: Peter and Jerry

1. *What is Peter's station in life? How does he compare with Jerry?*
Peter is married with two daughters, cats, two parakeets, two TVs, and he lives in a respectable neighborhood (the upper East Side). He earns good money ($18,000 was a lot back then!) working as an executive for a textbook publisher. In terms of social achievements he is a perfect example of the successful upper middle-class American. He belongs to the "haves".

Jerry, on the contrary, owns two empty picture frames, two pieces of rock, and a few "please letters". He has a room in a cheap rooming house situated in a poor area (the West Side), and run by a repulsive landlady with a vicious dog. His neighbors are social outsiders. In the eyes of society he is a loser, a "have not" (cf. **58** 30–**59** 28).

2. *Let's look at the essential differences between the two men with regard to their character and behavior.*
Peter acts politely, conventionally, though not sincerely (**55** 27). He is conservative, his ideas are shaped by *Time* magazine. His "Why, certainly [I'm married]" and "naturally, every man wants a son" (**56** 1, 11) attitude shows that he has no individual integrity. Peter is, in fact, extremely narrow-minded and tends to get patronizing (**58** 3). He does not seem to accept his age, but cultivates a younger look (cf. **54** 5–6). Peter believes in appearances and sometimes jumps to conclusions.

Jerry has a "great weariness" (**54** 11–12) about him. He is carelessly dressed, does not seem to believe in appearances. Jerry is rather obtrusive and does not act according to convention. He talks about things the way he sees them, badly wants communication and compassion, and can become aggressive (**69** 37). Jerry is a non-conformist, but more interesting than Peter, who is extremely predictable. He is distressed about his unhappy childhood (he lost his parents when he was ten). He has difficulties with women and has homosexual tendencies (**60** 25–**61** 2).

A selection of adjectives characterizing the two could be listed on the blackboard:

| **Jerry** | **Peter** |
|---|---|
| abnormal | normal |
| failure | success |
| no money | much money |
| poor address | good address |
| no family | standard family |
| not established | established |

| | |
|---|---|
| impolite | polite |
| crude | sophisticated |
| direct | indirect |
| avoids euphemisms | uses euphemisms |
| talkative, expressive | reticent, unexpressive |
| full of thoughts | has few thoughts |
| original, interesting | unoriginal, boring |

3. *Analyze this characterization with regard to the author's intentions and leanings.*
Albee defines Peter using negatives at the very beginning of the play: he is "neither fat nor gaunt, neither handsome nor homely" (**54** 3–4). He makes him a rather average, pale figure. By depicting Peter – the perfect personification of an American success story – in purely negative terms, he disqualifies the values and achievements Peter stands for.

(Note: Although Albee clearly favors Jerry, reactions to the play will vary according to the students' background.)

## Third Unit: Making Contact

1. *Describe Jerry's attempt to establish a relationship with his landlady's dog. Explain the significance of this parable* (**63** 4–**67** 36) *for Jerry's behavior toward Peter.*
First Jerry is kind, then he tries to kill the dog. In the end there is some kind of eye-to-eye contact, as Jerry and the dog "regard each other with a mixture of sadness and suspicion, and then [...] feign indifference" (**67** 14–15). But what Jerry has gained ("solitary free passage" **67** 20) is also a loss. Jerry's attempts to establish contact with the dog have failed; even the dog's previous aggressiveness had been preferable as this had at least been an attempt to reach out to the other. Neither love nor hate had been successful strategies. The two combined are "the teaching emotion" (**67** 24), i. e. the attitude that will teach the other. The other will have to be forced to enter into contact by a combination of love and hurt.

Jerry applies this lesson to his further interaction with Peter, first tickling him and then trying to force him to give up his bench by poking and punching him.

2. *What has Jerry learned in the zoo and how does he apply what he has learned?* (**69** 16–22)
He has learned that "everyone [is] separated by bars from everyone else

[...] But, if it's a zoo, that's the way it is" (**69** 20–22). Consequently he does not expect an easy "break-through" with Peter. He is prepared to violently burst the bars between them (which would explain Jerry's frequent references to something Peter will find in the papers, and his admission that he might have planned his own end).

**Homework**
Try to interpret the ending of the play in an essay. What could have been the playwright's intention? Is the play nothing but "a failed homosexual pass", as was suggested by one critic? Is Jerry some kind of "Messiah" who delivers Peter from his isolation, as was suggested by another critic? What does the play mean to *you*?

## Fourth Unit: The Ending of the Play

1. *Try to explain the ending of the play.*
(Note: We suggest listening to the poignant recording of the end of the play on cassette before discussing the ending.)

Jerry is clearly too hostile and generally weird to represent the Savior, but he is too sensitive and serious to be just a sex-maniac. Albee has said of him, "My hero is not a beatnik and he is not insane. He is over-sane. Though he dies, he passes on an awareness of life to the other character in the play."

Albee suggests that, although Jerry has finally succeeded in establishing a relationship, no matter how absurd this may be, it is Peter who really profits in this interaction. He was rudely shocked out of his complacency. And the shock had to be severe to get a person like him to change his ways.

But then again, people like Peter are not very likely to really change; they are more likely to go on repressing the experience. Albee's having Jerry point past the audience when he asks Peter "Is that Fifth Avenue?" (**54** 28) is perhaps an early indication of the playwright's intention to identify the audience with Fifth Avenue and the materialism and superficiality it connotes. Therefore, he might want the audience, rather than the surviving protagonist, to awaken from their blind indifference.

2. *Would you consider this play an absurd play?*
Not really, as the absurd condition of Jerry's and Peter's environment is not an a priori condition, but is made absurd by the people themselves: Peter, who declares he is a grownup and at the same time childishly insists

on his right to the bench, illustrates the absurdity of which he is capable. Allowing himself to get so overexcited about such a minor threat shows how caught up he is in his own little world, which must be terribly lacking in important problems. **(70).**

Jerry, for all his non-conformism, is not half as absurd as Peter, as he seems to be in control of the situation. He has seen through Peter's façade and tries to change things. He is there to show how absurd Peter is, not to function as a model.

**Homework**
How do you interpret the references to God and Christianity that are made throughout the text? (Answers are suggested in the analysis above, cf. pp. 123–124)

## For Further Study and Discussion

1. The Theatre of the Absurd: To further examine *The Zoo Story's* affiliation with the genre of the Theatre of the Absurd, students must agree upon a definition. We suggest Ionesco's understanding of the term, defined in an essay on Kafka: "Absurd is that which is devoid of purpose. [...] Cut off from his religious, metaphysical, and transcendental roots, man is lost; all his actions become senseless, absurd, useless."[6]

Try to explain what historical, social or psychological situation supports and generates such a literary development. Would you say that Albee's play fulfills the criteria mentioned by Ionesco?

The following quotations may give some suggestions:

In Europe many examples of the Theatre of the Absurd can be found (e.g. Samuel Beckett, Eugène Ionesco, Jean Genet) as "the convention of the Absurd springs from a feeling of deep disillusionment, the draining away of the sense of meaning and purpose in life, which has been characteristic of countries like France and Britain in the years after the Second World War. In the United States there has been no corresponding loss of meaning and purpose. The American dream of the 'Good life' is still very strong. In the United States the belief in progress that characterized Europe in the

---

6 Quoted in Martin Esslin, *The Theatre of the Absurd,* Revised and enlarged edition, Harmondsworth 1972, p. 23.

nineteenth century has been maintained into the middle of the twentieth. There have been signs, particulary since the shock administered by the Russian successes in the space race, that disillusion and frustration might become a factor in the American scene, but the rise of phenomena like the beat generation has been marginal compared to parallel developments in Europe."[7]

Esslin says about Edward Albee that he "comes into the category of the Theatre of the Absurd precisely because his work attacks the very foundation of American optimism. His first play, *The Zoo Story* (1958), which shared the bill at the Provincetown Playhouse with Beckett's *Krapp's Last Tape* already showed the forcefulness and bitter irony of his approach. [...]

Albee [later] produced a play that clearly takes up the style and subject matter of the Theatre of the Absurd and translates it into a genuine American idiom: *The American Dream* [...] attacks the ideals of progress, optimism, and faith in the national mission."[8]

In an article which originally appeared in *The New York Times Magazine* in 1962, Albee made the following remark on the Theatre of the Absurd: "I would submit that it is this latter attitude – that the theatre is a place to relax and have a good time – in conflict with the purpose of The Theatre of the Absurd – which is to make a man face up to the human condition as it really is – that has produced all the brouhaha and the dissent. I would submit that The Theatre of the Absurd, in the sense that it is truly the contemporary theatre, facing as it does man's condition as it is, is the Realistic theatre of our time; and that the supposed Realistic theatre – the term used here to mean most of what is done on Broadway – in the sense that it panders to the public need for self-congratulation and reassurance and presents a false picture of ourselves to ourselves, is, with an occasional very lovely exception, really and truly The Theatre of the Absurd."[9]

2. Comparative reading: Read Albee's *The American Dream,* a play he wrote shortly after writing *The Zoo Story,* and comment on how it might shed light on the earlier play.

---

7 *Ibid.* p. 301

8 *Ibid.* p. 302

9 Edward Albee, "Which Theatre is the Absurd One?" in: Horst Frenz, ed., *American Playwrights on Drama,* New York 1965, p. 172.

3. Biographical approach: Find out as much as you can about Albee's life. Does your knowledge enable you to reach a deeper understanding of his art?

Comment on the following statement: "Aus dem biographischen Wissen um Albees Schwierigkeiten in der Beziehung zu seinen Adoptiveltern werden die in all seinen Dramen thematisierten Kommunikationsprobleme der Figuren in fiktionstranszendierender Sicht als dramatische Versuche der Externalisierung und Bewältigung privater Psychosen gedeutet."[10]

4. Compare the treatment of the American Dream theme in the four dramas. Express your preferences and perspectives with regard to the plays and the theme.

---

10 Martin Brunkhorst, "Albees Frühwerk im Kontext des absurden Theaters," *Literatur in Wissenschaft und Unterricht* 12, 1979, p. 310.

# Select Bibliography

## American Drama

Bernstein, Samuel. *The Strands Entwined: A New Direction in American Drama*. Boston, 1980.

Bigsby, C. W. E. *Confrontation and Commitment: A Study of Contemporary American Drama 1959–1966*. Columbus, 1967.

Bungert, Hans, ed. *Die amerikanische Literatur der Gegenwart: Aspekte und Tendenzen*. Stuttgart, 1977.

Downer, Alan S. *The American Theater Today*. New York, 1967.

Esslin, Martin. "New Playwrights in America: An Outsider's View." *Theater* 9, II (1978).

Frenz, Horst, ed. *American Playwrights on Drama*. New York, 1965.

Gottfried, Martin. *A Theater Divided: The Postwar American Stage*. Boston, 1969.

Gould, Jean. *Modern American Playwrights*. New York, 1966.

Jackson, E. M. "American Theater in the Sixties." *Players* 48 (1973), 236–249.

Kernan, Alvin B., ed. *The Modern American Theater: A Collection of Critical Essays*. Englewood Cliffs, 1967.

Miller, K. "Myth and the American Dream: O'Neill to Albee." *Modern Drama* VII (1964), 190–198.

Vinson, James, ed. *Contemporary Dramatists*. London, 1973.

## The One-Act Play

Kosok, Heinz. "Englische und amerikanische Kurzdramen im Englischunterricht der Oberstufe." *Die Neueren Sprachen* 64 (1965), 520–531.

Schik, Berthold. "Das Kurzdrama im Fremdsprachenunterricht." *Der fremdsprachliche Unterricht* 49 (1979), 16–27.

Schnetz, Diemut. *Der moderne Einakter: Eine poetologische Untersuchung*. Bern/München 1967.

## Murray Schisgal

Marowitz, Charles. "Introduction" to *New American Drama.* Harmondsworth, 1966, pp. 13–14.

Vinson, James, ed. *Contemporary Dramatists.* London, 1973 pp. 678–681.

## Thornton Wilder

Burbank, Rex. *Thornton Wilder.* New York (TUSAS 5), 1961.

Frenz, K. "The Reception of Thornton Wilder's Plays in Germany". *Modern Drama* 3 (1960), 123–137

Goldstein, Malcolm. *The Art of Thornton Wilder.* Lincoln, Nebraska, 1965.

Goldstone, Richard. *Thornton Wilder: An Intimate Portrait.* New York, 1975.

Greene, J. "The World of Thornton Wilder." *Thought* 37 (1962), 563–584.

Haberman, Donald. *The Plays of Thornton Wilder: A Critical Study.* Middletown, Conn., 1967.

Popper, P. "The Universe of Thornton Wilder." *Harpers* 1381 (1965), 72–78.

Simon, Linda. *Thornton Wilder: His World.* Garden City, 1979.

## Tennessee Williams

Hirsch, Foster. *A Portrait of the Artist: The Plays of Tennessee Williams.* London, 1979.

Lubbers, Klaus. "Tennessee Williams." In: Martin Christadler, ed., *Amerikanische Literatur der Gegenwart,* Stuttgart 1973, p. 433.

Presley, P. "The Search for Hope in the Plays of Tennessee Williams." *Mississippi Quarterly* 25 (1971), 31–43.

Spevack, Marvin. "Tennessee Williams: The Idea of the Theater." In: *Das Amerikanische Drama,* Darmstadt 1972.

Steen, Mike. *A Look at Tennessee Williams.* New York, 1969.

Szeliski, S. "Tennessee Williams and the Tragedy of Sensitivity." *Western Humanities Review* 20 (1966), 203–211.

Tharpe, Jac, ed. *Tennessee Williams: A Tribute.* Jackson, 1977.

Tischler, Nancy. *Tennessee Williams.* Austin, 1969.

Weales, Gerald. *Tennessee Williams.* Minneapolis, 1965.

## Edward Albee


Amacher, Richard. *Edward Albee* (Revised Edition). Boston, 1982.

Bennett, R. B. "Tragic Vision in *The Zoo Story.*" *Modern Drama* 20 (1977), 55–66.

Bigsby, C. W. E. *Albee.* Edinburgh, 1969.

Bigsby, C. W. E., ed. *Edward Albee. A Collection of Critical Essays.* Englewood Cliffs, N.J., 1975.

Force, W. M. "The *What* Story? Or, Who's at the Zoo?" *Costerus* 2 (1972), 71–82.

De La Fuente, Patricia, et. al., editors. *Edward Albee: Planned Wilderness.* Edinburgh, 1980.

Missey, J. "A McCullers Influence on Albee's *Zoo Story.*" *American Notes and Queries* 13 (1975), 121–123.

Phillips, K. "Albee and the Theater of the Absurd." *Tennessee Studies in Literature* 10 (1965), 73–80.

Rauter, Herbert. "Edward Albee", in: Martin Christadler, ed. *Amerikanische Literatur der Gegenwart.* Stuttgart, 1973, pp.488–505.

Rutenberg, Michael. *Edward Albee: Playwright in Protest.* New York, 1969.

Stenz, Anita Maria. *Edward Albee: The Poet of Loss.* Paris, The Hague, New York, 1978.

Zimbardo, Ruth. "Symbolism and Naturalism in Albee's *Zoo Story.*" *Twentieth Century Literature* 8 (1962), 10–17. (Reprinted in C. W. E. Bigsby, ed., *Edward Albee. A Collection of Critical Essays;* see above.)